BANNERS, BUNTINGS, GARLANDS

& Pennants

40 CREATIVE IDEAS USING PAPER, FABRIC & MORE

KATHY SHELDON AND
AMANDA CARESTIO

LARK
New York

New York

An Imprint of Sterling Publishing
1166 Avenue of the Americas
New York, NY 10036

ISBN 978-1-4547-0897-1

Distributed in Canada by Sterling Publishing
℅ Canadian Manda Group, 664 Annette Street
Toronto, Ontario, Canada M6S 2C8
Distributed in the United Kingdom by GMC Distribution Services
Castle Place, 166 High Street, Lewes, East Sussex, England BN7 1XU
Distributed in Australia by Capricorn Link (Australia) Pty. Ltd.
P.O. Box 704, Windsor, NSW 2756, Australia

For information about custom editions, special sales, and premium
and corporate purchases, please contact Sterling Special Sales
at 800-805-5489 or specialsales@sterlingpublishing.com.

Photography by Dana Willard
Illustrations by Orrin Lundgren
Additional cover graphics © Shutterstock

Manufactured in China

2 4 6 8 10 9 7 5 3 1

larkcrafts.com

CONTENTS

HANG SOME HAPPINESS

Just why do we love banners (and buntings and garlands and pennants)? It's simple, really—they make us happy! We feel cheerful as soon as we hang one. Tie up a garland and, *ta-da!* any space—dining room, kitchen, nursery, porch, or patio—suddenly looks warm and inviting.

If you're looking for projects for year-round celebrations, we've got you covered with plenty of ideas. You'll find glittery stars and painted pinecones for Christmas, banners to make a birthday special (including a mini one to decorate a cake), and a garland of falling rose petals to sprinkle romance over any room. But if, like us, you've got a permanent case of garland-itis, don't worry: We've got loads of projects you can leave up all year, just to add a bit of whimsy to any day. We've even got a shrink- plastic bunting necklace you can hang around your neck to celebrate yourself!

Some of these banners are super fast and easy to make and require little more in the way of skills than tying string or squeezing glue. If you've got more time and crafting experience, try out some of the sewing and crochet projects. With every project, we've provided step-by-step instructions, templates, and a list of the materials and tools needed. Our Banner Basics (page 2) will get you started with the materials and tools you'll need. Making garlands is a wonderful way to use up those scraps of paper, fabric, or yarn you've been hoarding—and substitutions are encouraged. Need to change a flower color from yellow to celestial blue to fit your wedding scheme? Go right ahead. If we used jute but you're in the mood for colorful ribbon instead, be our guest. It's your party.

And speaking of parties, the guest designers we invited to celebrate with us in this book have generously shared so many truly awesome projects. Check out Aimee Ray's lovely Flocked Feathers garland on page 57. Cathe Holden has contributed a little pennant you can mail as a greeting (page 59). Cynthia Shaffer's Hanging Lilies (page 11) will knock your socks off. And Dana Willard's Baby Bunting (page 39) will make you want to have another baby (well, okay, perhaps make this as a shower gift instead then). Jennifer Jessee has designed an elegant Mod Pod Garland (page 33) that's got mid-century cool, and Laura Howard (who seems to be her own little craft factory in the UK) has sent love in the form of the Cross-Stitch Hearts garland on page 31. In the "so cute!" category, Mollie Johanson, with her signature style, mixes wood and forest critters for a banner that will make you smile (page 41).

Which takes us back to our first point: banners (and buntings and garlands and pennants) are just plain cheerful. So turn the page and get ready to hang some happiness.

GETTING STARTED: BANNER BASICS

If you're looking to brighten up your space in a just few quick and easy steps, think beautiful banners, buntings, and garlands. No matter the season, a simple bunting can transform a room, a porch, or even a yard. The projects in this book are the culmination of a long love affair with garlands … both our homes are filled with them! And when it comes to garlands, simple is often best. You don't need to track down fancy supplies or master tough techniques in order to make ones that will wow you and your guests.

BASIC SUPPLIES & MATERIALS

The beauty of banners is that they're very scrap friendly, whether you're talking paper, fabric, yarn, or ribbon scraps. We've provided a Basic Banner-Making Kit (see right), which includes what you need to get started. Then in each project, you'll find a list of specific materials and tools under the heading What You Need. Take a look at it: You may find you already have everything you need to plunge in and start making the project. If not, use it to make your shopping list (yes, we are giving you permission to head to a craft store!).

Flip through the pages and you'll see that most of the projects in this book use the usual suspects in terms of materials: cotton prints, felt, embroidery floss, pretty papers and card stock, washi tape, bias tape, and more. But, just for fun, we've also included some more exotic items in the mix: balsa wood for a forest-themed banner (page 41), cookie cutters sprayed a vibrant shade (page 81), lovely finds from a day at the shore (page 77), and even shrink plastic (available at craft stores and online). Part of the fun of making a garland is getting creative with what you string up. Look around your house for inspiration or, outside on the ground for that matter: You never know what you can turn into garland!

BASIC BANNER-MAKING KIT

* Scissors
* Small curved scissors (such as manicure scissors)
* Fabric shears
* Sewing needles
* Embroidery needles
* Pins
* Thread
* Craft glue
* Tape
* Ruler
* Measuring tape

GETTING THE HANG OF IT

You've found the objects you'd like to use for a garland, but what do you use to hang them? You've got lots of good options: jute, baker's twine, yarn, ribbon, perle cotton or embroidery floss, bias tape, rope, and wire all work well. When choosing, consider the weight of the objects you'll be stringing and how you'd like them to hang. Yarn will give and stretch for a soft drape while wire will supply a strong, straight arrangement that can bear a substantial amount of weight. Want to give the appearance that your objects are floating? Try nylon fishing line or another clear substrate. Just remember to always include extra material on each end of your garland, as you'll use this material for hanging, and start off with more than you think you'll need just to be on the safe side. You can always clip the ends if you've got too much, but nothing is worse than getting to the final steps of making a gorgeous garland only to find your ribbon is a few inches short and you have to start over (or make *another* trip to the craft store!).

HELPFUL TOOLS

Look to each set of project instructions for a full list of tools needed for that project. Again, you probably already have most of them: scissors, fabric shears, pencil, ruler, pins, needles, and thread. A few of the sewing projects call for a sewing machine, but only a few. You'll likely want some foam brushes at your disposal for painting and gluing applications. For the paper projects, have a craft knife and a hole punch on hand. For the crochet projects, you'll need a yarn or tapestry needle and crochet hooks in a few different sizes. You'll need wire cutters, flat-nose pliers, or shrink plastic for some of the other projects.

TECHNIQUES TO KNOW

Again, we promise, nothing too complicated here. Before you start, give the instructions a quick read to see if there's anything tricky to note, but the projects in this book are designed to be both beautiful and beginner friendly. A little painting and stamping, some simple machine sewing or hand stitching, and basic paper crafting are all you need. We've provided step-by-step instructions to guide you as you go. Our one jewelry project, the Shrink Plastic Bunting Necklace (page 91), uses only the most basic jewelry-making knowledge, opening and closing a jump ring, and we'll teach you that when you get there. A few projects include basic embroidery stitches and crochet stitches. We've included charts for them on pages 4–7 so you have the info you need on hand.

TRANSFERRING TEMPLATES

You'll find all the templates starting on page 102. We use various methods to transfer templates, depending on the complexity of the shapes and the material we're working with. For simple shapes, it's easiest just to photocopy the template (enlarging it if needed), cut it out, and trace around it. When transferring a template to felt, especially dark felt, we like to trace the template onto the shiny side of freezer paper (available in grocery stores) and then iron the paper onto the felt (waxy side down). We cut through the paper and felt at the same time, remove the paper, and have a shape with nice crisp and accurate cuts. Some of the projects call for embroidery patterns; and if we are transferring these to darker material, we usually trace the pattern onto a piece of tissue paper, pin the tissue in place on the material to be embroidered, and then embroider the designs right through both the tissue and the fabric below. When finished, we carefully tear away the tissue paper.

EMBROIDERY AND HAND-SEWING STITCHES

For some of the projects in this book, you'll need to know a few basic stitches.
Use these illustrations to refresh your memory or help you with any unfamiliar stitches.

STRAIGHT (OR RUNNING) STITCH Make this stitch by weaving the needle through the fabric at evenly spaced intervals.

FRENCH KNOT This elegant little knot adds interest and texture when embroidering or embellishing.

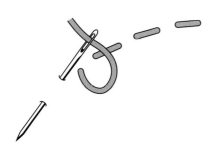

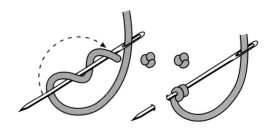

SCALLOP STITCH Scallop stitches are great for making flowers, borders, or smiles. Make a loose stitch from A to B and press it flat to one side with your finger. Bring the needle to the front of the fabric at C, inside the loop. Insert the needle at the outside of the stitch, at D, to hold it in place.

CROSS-STITCH Start by making a straight stitch from A to B. Make a second straight stitch from C to D. If you're making a row of cross stitches, you can first make a row of the underlying stitches (A to B) and then go back and cross them all at once.

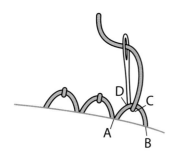

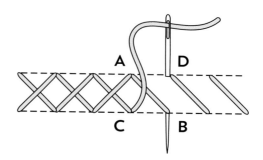

BLANKET STITCH   The blanket stitch is both decorative and functional. Use this stitch to accentuate an edge or to attach an appliqué.

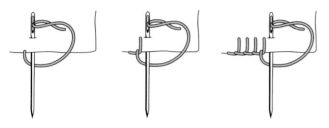

OVERHAND KNOT   Make a loop in the rope or twine, insert one end into the loop, and then pull on both ends to tighten the knot.

WHIPSTITCH   Also called the overcast stitch, the whipstitch is used to bind edges to prevent raveling or for decorative purposes. Simply stitch over the edge of the fabric.

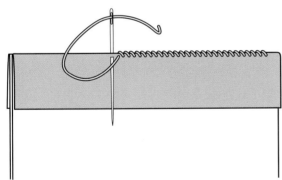

COW HITCH   The cow hitch is a quick way to add double strands of ribbon to a length of stringing material. Fold the ribbon in half to find its middle, and then loop the middle up and over the stringing material. Pull the two loose ends of ribbon up and through the loop. Pull the strands to tighten the knot.

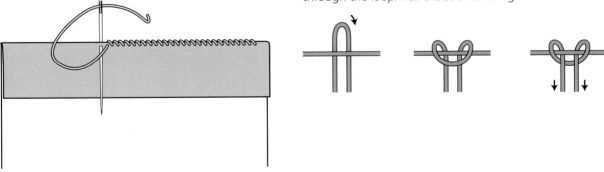

CROCHET STITCHES

Crocheted banners are lovely in and of themselves, but simple crochet is also a great way to add interest to your fabric banner projects. Three projects in this book use these basic stitches. We've included them here as a refresher.

CHAIN STITCH (CH)   Yarn over and draw the loop through.

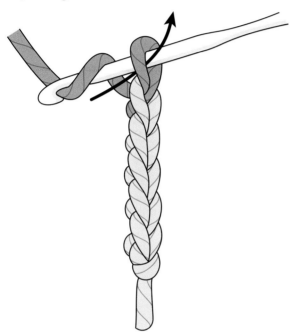

SINGLE CROCHET (SC)   Insert your hook through the work, yarn over, pull the loop through the work, yarn over, and pull the loop through both loops on your hook.

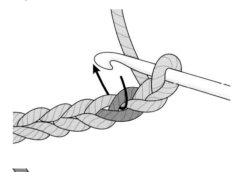

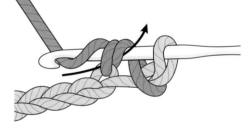

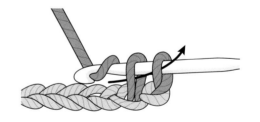

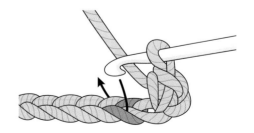

SLIP STITCH (SLST)   Insert your hook through the work, yarn over, and pull the loop through both the work and the loop on your hook.

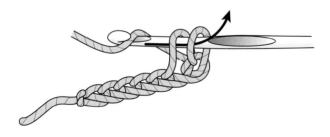

. . . .

DOUBLE CROCHET (DC) Yarn over, insert your hook through the work, yarn over, pull the loop through the work, yarn over, pull the loop through the first two loops on your hook, yarn over, and pull the loop through the final two loops on your hook.

1.

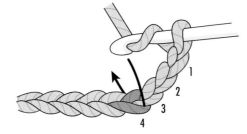

2.

3.

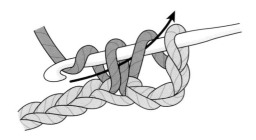

4.

5.

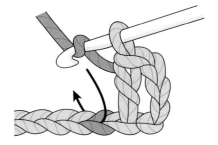

PAPER

HANGING LILIES

Large, delicate curled paper petals bring dimension to this floral-inspired garland. Hang several strands above a doorway or table setting for a bit of soft drama.

DESIGNER: CYNTHIA SHAFFER

WHAT YOU NEED
* Basic Banner-Making Kit (page 2)
* Templates (page 110)
* Permanent spray adhesive
* 12 sheets of 12- × 12-inch (30.1 cm × 30.1 cm) paper in coordinating prints
* Pencil
* Stylus or small crochet hook
* White glue
* Hot glue gun and glue sticks
* 10 yards (9.1 m) fishing line
* 24 white plastic beads

WHAT YOU DO

1. Apply spray adhesive to the wrong side of one of the printed papers and then adhere it to another paper, wrong sides facing.

NOTE: *The project shown paired one large-print paper with a smaller-print paper.*

2. Both flower templates will fit on a 12 × 12 (30.1 cm × 30.1 cm) paper. Using a pencil, trace the large flower template onto the paper by aligning one of the straight edges of the template with a straight edge of the paper. Repeat for the smaller flower template.

3. Trace the stamen templates onto the paper. Trace the longer stamen two times and the shorter stamen four times. Each flower will get one long and two short stamens.

4. Cut out all the traced shapes.

5. Use the stylus or crochet hook to score the flowers along the small flap that is indicated on the template. Fold the flap toward the small print for the large flower and toward the large print for the small flower.

6. Stack one short stamen, one long stamen, and then another short stamen, and glue them together at their squared off ends. Bend each short stamen slightly away from the long, center stamen. Set aside to dry. Repeat for the other set of stamens.

7. Using hot glue, adhere each stamen set to a flower. For the large flower, glue the stamen 2 inches (5.1 cm) from the small cut-out half-circle and on the smaller print side. For the smaller flower, glue the stamen ½ inch (1.3 cm) from the small cut-out half-circle and on the larger print side.

8. Gently roll the flowers to form a cone. Place a line of hot glue onto the small flap and then overlap the flower, carefully pressing the flower together. Repeat for the other flower.

9. Cut a length of fishing line that measures 3 yards (1 m). Tie one of the beads to the end of the fishing line. Insert the other end of the fishing line into the flower until the bead is pulled up and into the center of the flower.

10. Tie another bead to the fishing line, 4½ inches (11.4 cm) from the hole of the previous flower. Insert the other end of the fishing line into the flower until the bead is pulled up and into the center of the flower.

11. Repeat the above instructions to make the remaining 22 flowers.

PAPER CLOTHESLINE GARLAND

Pretty papers and mini clothespins create a delightful little wardrobe on the line.

PAPER CLOTHESLINE GARLAND

DESIGNER: LAURA HOWARD

WHAT YOU NEED
* Basic Banner-Making Kit (page 2)
* Templates (page 118)
* Pencil
* Eraser
* Card stock or paper in assorted colors
* Glue Stick
* String
* Mini clothespins
* *Optional:* washi tape in bright colors

WHAT YOU DO

1. Use the templates to make the apron, leggings, skirt, tights, jeans, and socks, using a selection of colors for the different clothes. Cut out each shape, then carefully use an eraser to remove any remaining pencil lines. Remember to make the socks in matching pairs!

2. Draw and cut out two matching pockets for the jeans, using the jean pocket template. Erase any pencil lines, then glue the pockets to the jeans.

3. To make the T-shirt, tank top, sweater, and dress, use the front templates and a pencil to trace the main garment shapes onto pieces of card stock or paper, using a selection of colors for the different clothes. Cut out each shape, then carefully use an eraser to remove any remaining pencil lines.

4. Trace along the top edge of the back templates using a pencil. Trace each shape onto the same color card stock or paper as used for the matching front shape. Make sure you leave enough room to add the front shapes in the next step.

5. Glue the front shapes onto the backing card stock, lining up the top edge of the card stock shapes with the pencil lines. When the glue has dried, cut the garments out again—this time cutting along the back necklines drawn in step 4. Erase any remaining pencil lines.

6. Draw and cut out a pocket using the tank top pocket template. This could be in matching or contrasting card stock or paper. Erase any pencil lines, then glue the pocket to the tank top, as pictured.

7. To make striped clothes, cut a piece of colored washi tape slightly wider than the garment you want to decorate. Then carefully cut along the middle of the piece of tape, cutting it in half lengthwise. Glue the narrow pieces of tape to the front of the garments (the main or "front" shape), creating a striped pattern. Turn the shape over and trim away the excess tape from the sides.

8. Repeat step 7 to cover the whole garment with stripes. Then follow the appropriate steps above to construct the rest of the garment, adding pockets and/or a back layer as required.

9. To construct the garland, simply use mini clothespins to clip the clothes to a string "clothesline" in your desired length.

TIP: *Instead of using tape to decorate the clothes, you can use patterned paper or draw your own patterns with pens, colored pencils, or rubber-stamped designs.*

BALL & CHAIN

Just a bit of stitch magic can turn simple circles into three-dimensional balls ... and a garland that shouts happy!

DESIGNER: DANA WILLARD

WHAT YOU NEED
* Basic Banner-Making Kit (page 2)
* Colorful papers
* Scissors or 3-inch- (7.6 cm) diameter circle paper punch
* Sewing machine
* Thread

WHAT YOU DO

1. Select shades and amount of paper. Six pieces of standard-weight paper per ball works well. Less paper is too sparse. More paper is harder to sew in your machine.

2. Use any round object to trace circles, then cut with scissors or a paper punch.

3. Carefully stack six circles for each ball, arranging the stacks in desired order. Start with a long tail of thread (so you can hang them from the ceiling) and sew the first stack of six circles right down the middle. Then sew the next stack of circles after that, then line up another stack and sew, and so on.

4. Fold the top circle in half around the sewn line. Do the same with all the circles, folding the last circle toward the back.

5. Continue to fold all the balls until you have a pretty paper ball chain of color!

ABC BUNTING

Create the whole alphabet for the nursery or spell a special message. All you need is printed papers and mini clothespins.

DESIGNER: KATHY SHELDON

WHAT YOU NEED

* Basic Banner-Making Kit (page 2)
* Templates (page 102)
* Small, sharp scissors
* Card stock in a variety of colors and patterns
* 10 feet (3 m) blue-and-white baker's twine
* Miniature clothespins

NOTE: *Since this garland contains small parts and string, hang it securely well out of the reach of babies or toddlers.*

WHAT YOU DO

1. Cut the cardstock into 26 5- × 5-inch (12.7 cm × 12.7 cm) squares. Place them in a line from left to right to find a pleasing arrangement of colors and patterns.

2. Use the templates to cut each letter from a cardstock square following the arrangement determined in step 1.

TIP: *For smooth edges, cut in a slow, continuous motion and always turn the paper, not the scissors. To cut out interior shapes, poke a small hole in the center, make several cuts from that hole to the inner border, and then carefully cut out along the inner border.*

3. Hang the baker's twine securely. Attach each letter with one or two miniature clothespins.

PAPER CUT PEAKS

A string of snow-capped mountains is simple to create with basic paper-cutting techniques. Make a strand in white or other mountain-themed colors.

DESIGNER: AMANDA CARESTIO

WHAT YOU NEED

* Basic Banner-Making Kit (page 2)
* Template (page 106)
* 8½- × 11-inch (21.6 cm × 28 cm) sheet heavy card stock
* Pencil
* Cutting mat
* Craft knife
* Metal ruler
* ⅛-inch (0.4 cm) hole punch
* Baker's twine
* Tape or craft glue

WHAT YOU DO

1. Trace the template onto the back of the card stock five times using a pencil. If you like, vary the shape of the snowdrift points to make your mountains slightly different.

2. Working on your cutting mat, cut the shapes out with the craft knife. Use the metal ruler as a guide to cut the straight edges.

3. Once all the shapes are cut, punch two holes, one at each side of the top of the mountain, about 1½ inches (1.3 cm) below the peak.

4. Cut a strand of baker's twine. Thread the baker's twine through the holes, spacing the mountains about 4 inches (10.2 cm) apart, and tape or glue the mountains in place.

5. Tie a knotted loop at each end of the baker's twine for hanging.

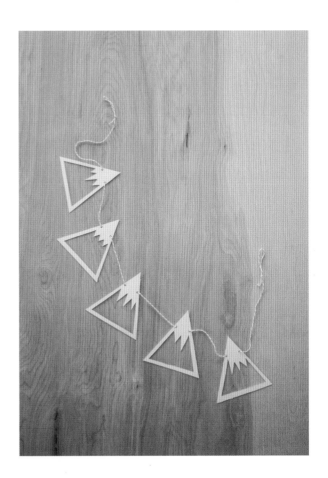

PAPER PETALS

Create these cascading blooms with pretty patterned paper and a simple origami folding pattern.

DESIGNER: AMANDA CARESTIO

WHAT YOU NEED
* Basic Banner-Making Kit (page 2)
* Patterned card stock
* Bone folder or spoon
* Craft glue
* Paperclips
* 52 inches (132 cm) yarn
* Tapestry needle

WHAT YOU DO

1. Cut the card stock into eight 4-inch (10.2 cm) squares.

2. To make a flower, fold the square in half diagonally so that two opposite points come together (and you've created a triangle). Fold the left and right corners over the center point to create the left and right petals. Go over all the folds with a bone folder or spoon.

3. Glue the petals together where they overlap. Paperclip the layers together while the glue dries. Repeat to make eight flowers.

4. For the strands with two flowers, cut a 12-inch (30.1 cm) piece of yarn. Knot the end, thread the yarn onto the tapestry needle, and push the needle up through the first flower, in the small opening between the left and right petals, up to the knot. Make another knot in the yarn, about 4 inches (10.2 cm) above the first petal, and string on another petal, again up to the knot. Repeat to make two more two-flower strands.

5. For the strands with one flower, cut a 9-inch (22.9 cm) piece of yarn. Knot the end, thread the yarn onto the yarn needle, and push the needle up through the flower, in the small opening between the left and right petals, up to the knot.

6. Cut two 20-inch (0.5 m) strands of yarn. Tie the two- and one-flower strands (alternating as you go) onto the double strands, spacing them about 3 inches (7.6 cm) apart.

DIAMOND STRANDS

A collection of colorful paint chips gets an upgrade! Cut a stack of paint samples in your favorite shades to create a simple diamond silhouette.

DESIGNER: CYNTHIA SHAFFER

WHAT YOU NEED
* Basic Banner-Making Kit (page 2)
* Template (page 105)
* Seven 5- × 6-inch (12.7 cm × 15.2 cm) paint chips in colors of your choice
* Pencil
* ⅛-inch (0.4 cm) hole punch
* 2½ yards white baker's twine

WHAT YOU DO

1. Line up the top edge of the diamond template with the top edge of the paint chip. Trace the template and transfer the two circles for holes.

2. Cut out the diamond shape, and then using the hole punch, punch out the small holes where the twine will be threaded.

3. Repeat for all the paint chips.

4. Line the diamond shapes up in the order that they are to be hung, then weave the baker's twine in and out of the holes.

5. Slide the diamond shapes along the twine, spacing them evenly.

FESTIVE FAN BUNTING

Floral wrapping paper plus some simple fan folds make for one fun bunting.

DESIGNER: KATHY SHELDON

WHAT YOU NEED

* Basic Banner-Making Kit (page 2)
* Two 12- × 12-inch (30.5 cm × 30.5 cm) sheets colored paper
* 1 roll floral wrapping paper
* ⅞ inch × 3 to 4 yards (.9 cm × 2.7 m to 3.7 m) ribbon
* Pencil
* Glue
* Stapler

WHAT YOU DO

1. Cut each sheet of colored paper (orange in the project shown) in half to get four 6- × 12-inch (15.3 cm × 30.5 cm) strips. This will give you one more than you need, so you can mess up on your first try! With the paper colored side up, fold accordion-style pleats down the 12-inch (30.5 cm) length, making each pleat about 1-inch (2.5 cm) deep. Keep the edges of the paper carefully aligned as you fold. When finished, you should have a 6-inch (15.2 cm) strip of folded paper. Repeat with two more strips of paper, then set them all aside.

2. Cut one 12- × 18-inch (30.5 cm × 45.7 cm) rectangle from the floral wrapping paper. Fold the paper accordion-style down the 18-inch (45.7 cm) length, making each pleat about 1½ inches (3.8 cm) deep. Keep the edges of the paper carefully aligned as you fold. When finished, you should have a 12-inch (30.5 cm) strip of folded paper. Repeat with three more 12- × 18-inch (30.8 cm × 45.7 cm) strips of floral paper, and then set them all aside.

3. The decorated section of the bunting will be approximately 6 feet (1.8 m) across. Decide how much ribbon you'll need on each end for hanging, then trim the ribbon if necessary. Fold the ribbon in half lengthwise to find its center, and mark it with a pencil on the side you want to have facing up on the completed bunting.

4. Center one short edge of one solid-color accordion-folded strip over the mark at the center of the ribbon, so the top side of the fold faces up and the rest of the pleated paper hangs down with the colored side facing out. Coat the back of the top fold with glue and attach it to the ribbon. Let the glue dry.

5. Gather the pleats in the paper strip (with the ribbon inside the top fold) and then fold the strip in half across its 6-inch (15.3 cm) length. Staple close to the fold, making sure to pierce all of the paper folds and the ribbon.

6. Open up the folds and glue the bottom open ends together to form a paper fan.

7. Repeat steps 4 to 6 to add the remaining fans to either side of the center fan, using the photo for reference, and spacing each fan about ¾ inch (1.9 cm) apart. The top edge of each larger fan will be wider than the ribbon—just fold it around to the back of the ribbon and glue it. Because these fans are wider, you may also need to staple across the top edge twice.

8. Hang your garland and cut any excess ribbon. The fans will fold nicely when the time comes to store your garland away.

BOTANICAL BEAUTIES

Cut a few favorite vintage illustrations from an old book, then frame them in a row on paper coasters and ribbon.

DESIGNER: AMANDA CARESTIO

WHAT YOU NEED
* Basic Banner-Making Kit (page 2)
* Glass cup
* Paper coasters
* 5 illustrations from a vintage book
* Pencil
* Craft glue
* 40- to 50-inch (1 m to 1.3 m) length ribbon
* Tape

WHAT YOU DO

1. Pick a glass cup that will work with the size of your paper coasters. Place the cup over the illustrations and trace around the edge.

2. Cut around the illustration, using the traced line from step 1. Repeat for the other illustrations.

3. Run a thin bead of craft glue around the backside of the illustrations and place one in the center of each coaster. If needed, place the coasters between the pages of a book to make sure the layers dry flat.

4. Cut the ribbon and fold it in half. Position and then tape the coasters in place on the double strand of ribbon, placing them about 3 inches (7.6 cm) apart. Turn the bunting over and glue the ribbon in place on the back of the coasters.

5. Trim the ribbon ends at the end of the bunting.

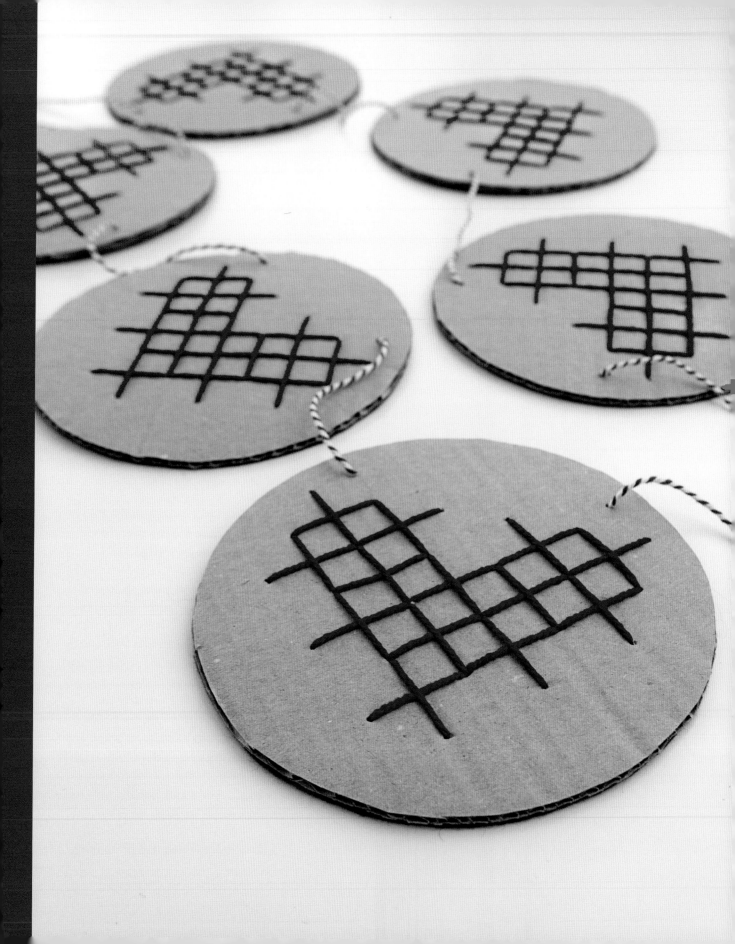

CROSS-STITCH HEARTS

Simple hearts stitched on cardboard medallions . . . how we love thee! A garland in every color, please.

DESIGNER: LAURA HOWARD

WHAT YOU NEED

* Basic Banner-Making Kit (page 2)
* Template (page 105)
* Pencil
* Scrap card stock (or any thick paper)
* Brown corrugated cardboard
* Craft mat
* Compass (or other implement with a sharp point)
* Large, sharp sewing needle
* Red yarn
* *Optional:* PVA glue and red felt (slightly larger than the circle template)

WHAT YOU DO

1. Use the template to draw a circle on a piece of scrap card stock and cut it out.

2. Using this card stock template and a pencil, trace a circle onto the back of the corrugated cardboard. Cut out a corrugated cardboard circle and turn it over.

3. Place the cardboard circle on a craft mat to protect your work surface, and place the card stock template on top, lining up the edges neatly. Using the dots on the template as a guide, one by one, poke through each dot with the point of the compass. Remove the template and set it aside, checking that you've completed the pattern of dots.

4. Use the large, sharp sewing needle to poke a hole through the cardboard at each point you've pricked with the compass, carefully passing the needle all the way through the cardboard from front to back.

5. Cut a long piece of red yarn and tie a large knot in one end, leaving a couple of inches (about 5 cm) of yarn tail below the knot. Thread the yarn onto the large needle and stitch the cross-stitch design, as pictured. Start and finish your stitching in the same place, knotting the two yarn ends together securely, then trimming away the excess yarn.

TIP: *Each X-shaped cross-stitch is made up of two single stitches. Sew all the stitches in one direction, then sew all the stitches in the other direction to create the pattern of crosses.*

6. (*Optional—required only if the back of your garland will be visible.*) Apply PVA craft glue to the back of the stitched circle. Adhere a piece of red felt to the back, pressing it firmly to the card. After it is dry, cut away the excess felt, leaving a neat circle of red felt on the back of the cardboard circle.

TIP: *For added neatness, press the cardboard and felt circles flat under a pile of heavy books, protecting the books with scrap paper.*

7. Repeat steps 2 to 6 to create lots of cross-stitched circles. For a neat finish, make sure your stitching is the same on each cross-stitch heart.

8. Use a large, sharp needle to carefully poke two holes in the top of each circle, approximately ½ inch (1.3 cm) from both the edge of the circle and the top of the heart.

9. Cut a long piece of red yarn and use it to thread the needle, then thread the circles onto the yarn one by one.

MOD POD GARLAND

Love all things mod? So do we! Create these simple mod pods with coordinating card stock layers.

DESIGNER: JENNIFER JESSEE

WHAT YOU NEED

* Basic Banner-Making Kit (page 2)
* Templates (page 107)
* Card stock: 6 sheets dark gray, 8 sheets light gray, 6 sheets coral, 6 sheets olive green, and 4 sheets pale olive green
* 8 to 10 feet (2.4 to 3 m) of dark gray cording
* Glue stick
* Burnishing tool, such as a bone folder

WHAT YOU DO

1. First, fold each sheet of card stock in half so you'll get two matching shapes each time you cut. Referring to the photos for color combinations, use the templates to cut each of the three larger and the three smaller shapes from the various colors of card stock. Cut as many shapes as needed for your chosen garland length, keeping in mind that each "mod pod" requires two large and two matching smaller shapes.

2. Fold your cording in half to mark the center and then open it back up. Using the photos for reference, sandwich the center of the cord between two large dark gray shapes and glue them together, burnishing lightly.

3. Glue one corresponding smaller light gray shape to the front of the dark gray shape and one to the back. Burnish lightly.

4. Repeat this process with other colors and sizes of large and small shapes to complete the garland, spacing each mod pod 1½ inches (3.8 cm) or so apart. Remember to leave tails at the end to tie your garland!

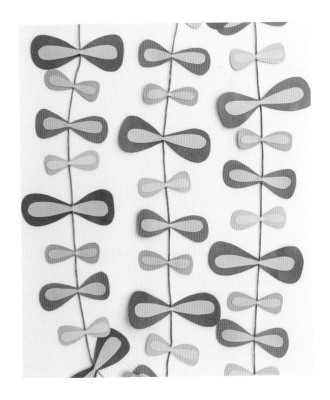

GLITTER STARS

Star light, star bright! Glitter paper, punched or cut stars, and jute combine for easy, rustic charm.

DESIGNER: KATHY SHELDON

WHAT YOU NEED

* Basic Banner-Making Kit (page 2)
* Template (page 105)
* Scissors, craft knife, or 3-inch [7.6 cm] star-shaped paper punch
* 12- × 12-inch (30.8 cm × 30.8 cm) sheets gold or silver glitter card stock
* $\frac{1}{16}$-inch (0.2 cm) hole punch
* 2 yards (1.8 m) twine, plus extra for hanging

WHAT YOU DO

1. Use the template and scissors or a craft knife, or use a star punch to cut 10 stars from the glitter cardstock.

2. Use the hole punch to make a hole in the center of each star's top point.

3. Starting with the first star on the left, leave a tail for hanging and then thread the twine through the star's hole and tie a simple knot in the twine, making sure the glitter side of the star is facing forward.

4. Measure approximately 4 inches (10.2 cm) to the right on the twine and add the second star. Repeat, measuring carefully each time, until all 10 stars are attached.

FABRIC

BABY BUNTING

Nothing brightens up a new nursery better than a cheery strand of classic bunting in sweet prints.

DESIGNER: DANA WILLARD

WHAT YOU NEED
* Basic Banner-Making Kit (page 2)
* Pencil
* Fabric in a variety of prints and patterns
* Plate or Bowl
* Sewing machine
* Thread
* Iron
* Double-fold bias tape, ½ inch × 3 yards (1.3 cm × 2.7 m)

WHAT YOU DO

1. Use something round—such as a plate or bowl—to trace and cut circles of fabric from a variety of fabric prints. Cut two layers of each fabric at the same time.

2. With right sides of the fabric together, sew two circles together all the way around using a ¼-inch (0.6 cm) seam allowance.

3. Clip small snips into the seam allowance to help the curved area lay flat.

4. Continue sewing circles together until you've made enough for the desired length of your bunting, keeping in mind that each circle will create two scallops.

5. Cut each finished circle in half. (The easiest way to do this is to fold each circle in half and press with a hot iron for a second to create a subtle crease. Then cut along that crease.)

6. Turn the semi-circles right side out and press with a hot iron.

7. Gather your bias tape. To first sew a tail to help you hang your bunting, start at one end of the bias tape and sew it closed by sewing down the side of the bias tape for about 6 inches (15.2 cm).

8. Grab your first semi-circle of fabric and sandwich it right between the two bias tape layers. Continue sewing down the bias tape (sewing the semi-circles of fabric in place).

9. Then grab another semi-circle, sandwich it inside the bias tape, and continue sewing.

10. Repeat with all the semi-circles. Then sew another 6-inch (15.2 cm) tail on the other end of the bias tape.

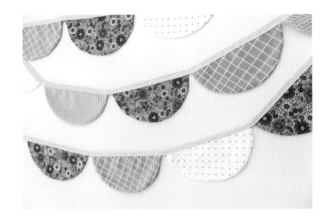

INTO THE WOODS

Journey along with a merry band of felt forest friends! Made with wood and simple stitched accents, this project is a great pick for crafting with kids.

DESIGNER: MOLLIE JOHANSON

WHAT YOU NEED

* Basic Banner-Making Kit (page 2)
* Templates (page 116)
* Drill with ³⁄₁₆-inch (4.8 cm) bit or a punch tool (see Tip A)
* 6 wood cut-out rectangles, 5 × 6 inches (12.7 × 15.2 cm) each
* 5 wood cut-out rectangles, 2½ × 3½ inches (6.4 × 8.9 cm) each
* Felt: reddish brown, red, white, tan, brown, dark green, and light green
* Pencil
* Freezer paper (see Tip B)
* Black embroidery floss
* Needle
* Fabric or craft glue
* Ribbon, ¼ inch × 6 feet (0.6 cm × 1.8 m)

WHAT YOU DO

1. Punch or drill ³⁄₁₆-inch (4.8 cm) holes in the top corners of the wood pieces.

TIP A: *If you aren't able to punch or drill the holes in the wood pieces, glue a looped tab of felt on the back of each piece.*

2. Cut out all of the felt pieces for each forest friend.

TIP B: *For easy cutting, trace the pieces onto freezer paper and iron the paper onto the felt. Cut through the paper and felt at the same time, then remove the paper.*

DEER: From reddish brown, cut one body and two legs.

TOADSTOOLS: From red, cut two toadstool caps. From white, cut two toadstool bases and six spots.

RABBIT: From tan, cut one body and four limbs. From white, cut one tail.

ACORNS: From tan, cut two acorn bottoms. From brown, cut two acorn caps.

BEAR: From brown, cut one body and four limbs.

TREES: From dark green, cut one small tree. From light green, cut one large tree.

SQUIRREL: From reddish brown, cut one body, one tail, and four limbs.

HEDGEHOG: From brown, cut one spine. From tan, cut one body and four limbs.

OWL: From brown, cut one body and two wings. From tan, cut one face.

3. Embroider the faces using three strands of black embroidery floss. Make French knots for the eyes, and use the satin stitch for the noses, the scallop stitch for the smiles, and the back stitch for all straight lines.

4. Use fabric glue to layer and attach the pieces to the wood, using the photos for placement, especially for the limbs.

5. Thread the ribbon through the holes in the wood pieces and tie a loop at each end for hanging.

CHALKBOARD FABRIC & BURLAP BUNTING

Use chalk on this chalkboard-fabric bunting to wish loved ones bon voyage, and then erase and rewrite to welcome them back home!

DESIGNER: KATHY SHELDON

WHAT YOU NEED

* Basic Banner-Making Kit (page 2)
* Templates (page 106)
* Burlap, 42 × 8 inches (1.1 m × 20.3 cm)
* Paper-back iron-on adhesive, 48 x 8 inches (1.1 m x 20.3 cm)
* Chalkboard fabric, 42 × 8 inches (1.1 m × 20.3 cm), (see Note)
* Iron
* Pencil
* ¼-inch (0.6 cm) hole punch
* Ribbon (or any stringing material of your choice)
* Chalk
* Damp Cloth

NOTE: *Chalkboard fabric is available at many fabric and crafts stores and online. Iron-on adhesive is used here to stiffen the burlap and keep it from fraying. Be sure to use the kind that isn't sticky unless it is heated.*

WHAT YOU DO

1. Place the burlap right side (or best side) down on an ironing board.

2. Place the paper-backed iron-on adhesive on the back of the burlap. Follow the manufacturer's directions to affix the adhesive, but do not remove the paper backing. Follow the manufacturer's directions to affix the adhesive, but do not remove the paper backing. You may need to use a slightly higher temperature than called for to get the adhesive to stick to the burlap.

3. Use the large triangle template and a pencil to trace 12 triangles (also tracing the circles for the two hanging holes) onto the paper backing—six across the top and six across the bottom.

4. Carefully cut out all 12 triangles. Use the hole punch to punch the hanging holes, and then remove the paper backing. The back of the triangles should now have a smooth, clear coating that isn't sticky.

5. Use the small triangle template to trace 12 triangles from the chalkboard fabric, including the circles for the two hanging holes. Use the hole punch to punch the hanging holes.

TIP: *Before writing on chalkboard fabric for the first time, "prime" it by rubbing the side of a chalk stick over the entire surface, first vertically and then horizontally. Wipe the fabric with a soft cloth and then repeat one more time.*

6. Place one chalkboard pennant on each burlap one, aligning the hanging holes. Thread the ribbon (from the back to the front and then out the back again) through the holes to hang all the pennants.

7. Use chalk to write your message. When it's time to erase, just use a slightly damp cloth and rub gently.

AUTUMN GARLAND

Celebrate fall with festive colors that stay! Simple stitched felt leaves are tucked among too-cute dimensional pinecones.

AUTUMN GARLAND

DESIGNER: LAURA HOWARD

WHAT YOU NEED

* Basic Banner-Making Kit (page 2)
* Templates (page 108)
* Felt: brown plus assorted autumnal shades
* Sewing needle and pins
* Sewing thread: matching brown plus matching autumnal shades
* Stuffing
* Embroidery floss in assorted autumnal shades
* White yarn
* Large, sharp sewing needle
* *Optional*: air-erasable fabric marker

WHAT YOU DO

TO MAKE THE PINECONES:

1. Use the templates to cut out two of each pinecone piece (the main shape and A through E) from the brown felt. Turn over one set of pieces and set aside—this will become the back of the pinecone.

2. Pin piece A to the bottom (pointed end) of the front pinecone piece, using the photo for placement and making sure the edges of the pieces align. Use matching brown sewing thread to sew it in place by taking one small stitch at the point between each scallop and inserting a line of the running stitch along the top edge. Then remove the pin.

3. Layer the rest of the pieces (B, C, D, and E) one by one, pinning then sewing them in place as in step 2. When sewing piece E, just sew the small stitches between the scallops—don't sew a line of the running stitch along the top edge.

4. Repeat steps 2 and 3 to sew the back of the pinecone.

5. Place the front and back of the pinecone together. Sew the edges together with brown thread using the blanket (or whip) stitch: Starting next to the stem, sew up around the stem, down one side of the pinecone, then back up the other side, leaving a gap for stuffing.

6. Stuff the pinecone lightly with the stuffing, leaving the stem unstuffed. Then sew up the gap with more brown thread and blanket (or whip) stitches.

7. Repeat steps 1 to 6 to create several plush pinecones.

TO MAKE THE LEAVES:

8. Use one of the leaf templates to cut out two leaf shapes from matching felt in an autumnal shade.

9. Cut a length of embroidery floss in a coordinating color and separate half the strands (for six-stranded floss, use three strands). Use this floss and the running stitch to sew "veins" on the front of the leaf, as pictured. Stitch these freehand, or draw lines with an air-erasable fabric marker, then stitch along the lines.

10. Place the decorated front and plain back of the leaf together and pin. Sew around the edges using the blanket (or whip) stitch in matching sewing thread, removing the pins as you sew.

11. Repeat steps 8 to 10 to create a selection of embroidered leaves in assorted colors.

TO CONSTRUCT THE GARLAND:

12. Arrange the pinecones and leaves in your desired order.

13. Cut a long piece of white yarn. Thread a large, sharp sewing needle and sew the felt shapes onto the yarn one by one, threading the yarn through the stems of the leaves and pinecones.

SWEET SCALLOPED PENNANTS

A scalloped, crocheted edge plus a mix of delicate floral prints from your stash equals one sweet stash-busting project!

DESIGNER: CYNTHIA SHAFFER

WHAT YOU NEED
(FOR ONE PENNANT)

* Basic Banner-Making Kit (page 2)
* Template (page 106)
* Print cotton fabric, 7 × 8 inches (17.8 cm × 20.3 cm)
* White cotton fabric, 7 × 8 inches (17.8 cm × 20.3 cm)
* Large-eye needle
* Perle cotton thread (#5) or cotton crochet thread
* Crochet hook: 2.75mm (size C-2)
* Light yellow single-fold bias tape, 11 inches (27.9 cm)
* Sewing Pins

WHAT YOU DO

1. Use the template to cut one triangle from the print cotton fabric and one from the white cotton fabric.

2. With right sides facing, pin then machine stitch two sides of the triangle with a ¼-inch (0.6 cm) seam allowance. Start stitching at the top right, pivoting at the bottom point and then continuing up the left side. Back tack at the beginning and the end of the stitching.

3. Trim the seam allowance at the bottom point.

4. Turn the triangle right sides out and press the triangle flat.

5. Using the large-eye needle and the perle cotton in a contrasting color, blanket stitch around the triangle along the stitched seams.

6. Using the perle cotton and the crochet hook, crochet a scalloped edge into the blanket stitch as follows: In the first blanket stitch, 2 single crochets (sc); in the next blanket stitch, 2 double crochets (dc); in the next blanket stitch, 2 dc. Repeat, ending with 2 sc in the last blanket stitch.

7. Fold the bias tape in half and mark the center with a pin. Fold the triangle in half and mark the center with a sewing pin.

8. Pin the bias tape to the pennant, encasing the top cut edge and matching the center pin marks.

9. Machine stitch the bias tape to the pennant.

10. Repeat steps 1 to 9 for the remaining pennants.

11. Tie the pennants together with a simple overhand knot. Arrange and rearrange the pennants to your personal liking or to match a particular room or setting.

HAPPY DAY

Brighten any day with this cheerful strand of stitched letters on felt. Switch up the colors and the ribbons to make the most of your stash. You can customize this banner for any occasion!

HAPPY DAY

DESIGNER: MOLLIE JOHANSON

WHAT YOU NEED

* Basic Banner-Making Kit (page 2)
* Templates (page 111)
* Iron
* Scissors
* Cotton fabric: color A (½ yard [0.5 m]), color B (½ yard [0.5 m] if making binding or ⅓ yard [30.1 cm] if using bias tape), color C (⅓ yard [30.1 cm]), and color D (⅓ yard [30.1 cm])
* Fusible midweight interfacing, 20 inches × 1 yard (0.5 m × 1 m)
* Pencil
* Embroidery floss: black and two coordinating colors
* Embroidery needle
* Pins
* Sewing machine
* Chopstick
* *Optional:* double-fold bias tape, 3 yards (1 m), rotary cutter, cutting mat, embroidery hoop

WHAT YOU DO

1. Iron the interfacing onto the back of fabric A. Cut out nine triangles and trace the letter motifs onto them with a pencil, tracing faces onto a few of the letters.

2. Embroider the designs with three stands of thread. Chain stitch the main outline, then outline a second time with the back stitch. Stitch the faces with French knots for the eyes and back stitch for the mouths (see photos on pages 52–53).

TIP: *Because the triangles are backed with interfacing, you may find the fabric is taut enough to stitch without stretching it over an embroidery hoop.*

3. Cut three triangles each from fabrics B, C, and D. Pin them to the embroidered triangles with right sides together. Arrange them so that they make a pattern of colors when the letters are in order.

4. Sew the two long sides of each triangle, leaving the top open. Clip the point of each pennant, then turn them right side out, poking the point with a chopstick. Press the seams.

5. If making your own binding, cut three 2- × 40-inch (5.1 cm × 1.1 m) strips of fabric B and join them to make one strip. Press the edges in to the center, then press the strip in half. Pin the pennants between the folded binding, spacing them 1¾ inches (4.4 cm) apart.

6. Sew the binding strip or bias tape to the pennants with matching thread, stitching close to the lower folded binding edge.

7. Cut ten 1- x 26-inch (2.5 cm x 0.7 m) strips each from fabrics C and D. Attach two strips next to each pennant, using a cow hitch (see page 5).

FAB FRINGE

Bye-bye, scraps! Simply cut your too-small fabric bits into strips and sew them to a strand of bias tape.

DESIGNER: DANA WILLARD

WHAT YOU NEED

* Basic Banner-Making Kit (page 2)
* Scraps of fabric
* Any color double-fold bias tape, ½ inch × 3 yards (1.3 cm × 0.9 m)
* Sewing thread in color that matches bias tape
* Fabric scissors

WHAT YOU DO

1. Fold a scrap of fabric in half (so you have two layers of fabric) and cut a square or rectangle of fabric approximately 2 × 3 inches (5.1 cm × 7.6 cm) or any size you like.

2. Repeat and cut more rectangle scraps until you have a nice stack of scraps. It's best to vary the sizes of your rectangles—cut some 2 × 3 inches (5.1 cm × 7.6 cm), others 1½ × 4 inches (3.8 cm × 10.2 cm), and so on.

3. Gather your bias tape. To first sew a tail to help you hang your bunting, start at one end of the bias tape and sew it closed by sewing down the side of the bias tape for about 6 inches (15.2 cm).

4. Grab your first scrap of fabric and sandwich it between the two bias tape layers. Continue sewing down the bias tape, sewing the scrap of fabric in place.

5. Grab another scrap, sandwich it inside the bias tape, and continue sewing. Repeat again and again until you've reached the desired length for your garland.

6. Sew another 6-inch tail on the other end of the bias tape.

7. Time to fringe your garland. Using a pair of fabric scissors, cut vertical lines in each of your scraps (about ¾ inch [1.9 cm] wide) to create fringe.

FLOCKED FEATHERS

Fun felt in pastel tones creates this simple feather-themed garland, perfect above a canvas tent, a summer fort, or any place daydreamers unwind.

DESIGNER: AIMEE RAY

WHAT YOU NEED

* Basic Banner-Making Kit (page 2)
* Templates (page 109)
* Felt: in a variety of browns, pinks, greens, grays, oranges (this is a great way to use up scraps!)
* Embroidery thread: brown, pink, green, and cream
* Embroidery needle
* Grosgrain ribbon, ⅝ inch × 5 feet (1.5 cm × 1.5 m)

WHAT YOU DO

1. Use the feather templates to cut out several long and short feathers from different colors of felt. Cut a center piece in a different color for each feather. Cut out ten large feathers and ten small feathers.

2. Cut notches or slits along the edges of each feather piece, or leave some plain.

3. Stitch the center pieces in place on each feather using the embroidery patterns provided.

4. Arrange the feathers in a row, varying sizes and colors. Stitch each feather to the ribbon using a cross-stitch at the top.

YOU ARE LOVED MINI BUNTING

Instead of sending a card, mail a mini celebration with this stamped-message mini bunting that can be wrapped around a card or cardstock and tucked in an envelope.

DESIGNER: CATHE HOLDEN

WHAT YOU NEED

* Basic Banner-Making Kit (page 2)
* Template (page 115)
* Solid-color cotton fabric scraps
* Alphabet rubber stamps (¾-inch [1.9 cm])
* Contrasting dye-based ink pad
* Scissors, or rotary cutter and cutting mat
* Sewing machine
* Coordinating thread
* Blank greeting card and envelope (4.5 × 6.25 inches [11.4 cm × 16 cm] folded)
* Washi tape

WHAT YOU DO

1. Place the template onto two pieces of stacked fabric and trim out along pattern edge, repeating with enough fabric pieces to spell out your banner, including spacer pennants and an additional two for the beginning and end of your finished bunting.

2. Rubber stamp one letter per triangle, ¼ inch (0.6 cm) from the top of each, to spell out your message.

3. Stack triangles in order, with the beginning of the message on top, including the blank starter pennant(s), one blank between each word, and the final blank on the bottom of the stack.

4. Trim the width of the folded greeting card a total of ⅛ inch to ¼ inch (0.4 cm to 0.6 cm) and add a written sentiment inside.

5. Pull a 6-inch (15.2 cm) length of thread from your sewing machine needle and bobbin before beginning your first stitch. Place the first triangle under the sewing foot and begin slowly stitching along the top of the triangle at ⅛-inch (0.4 cm) seam allowance. As you complete the stitching, place the next triangle under the foot, allowing it to feed in and attach next to the first triangle. Continue sewing until all pennants are attached. Pull the bunting from the machine with a 6-inch (15.2 cm) length of thread. To keep bunting from coming unstitched, cut the thread and knot the beginning two threads together at the start of the first pennant. Repeat with the ending threads.

6. Use a small piece of washi tape to attach the ending threads to the front or back of the folded greeting card, wrapping the bunting around until the beginning of the message is on the front. Secure beginning threads at the front of the card with washi tape.

7. Slide the bunting-wrapped greeting card into the envelope. Once the card is pulled from the envelope, the recipient can detach the beginning of the bunting, unwrap, and display.

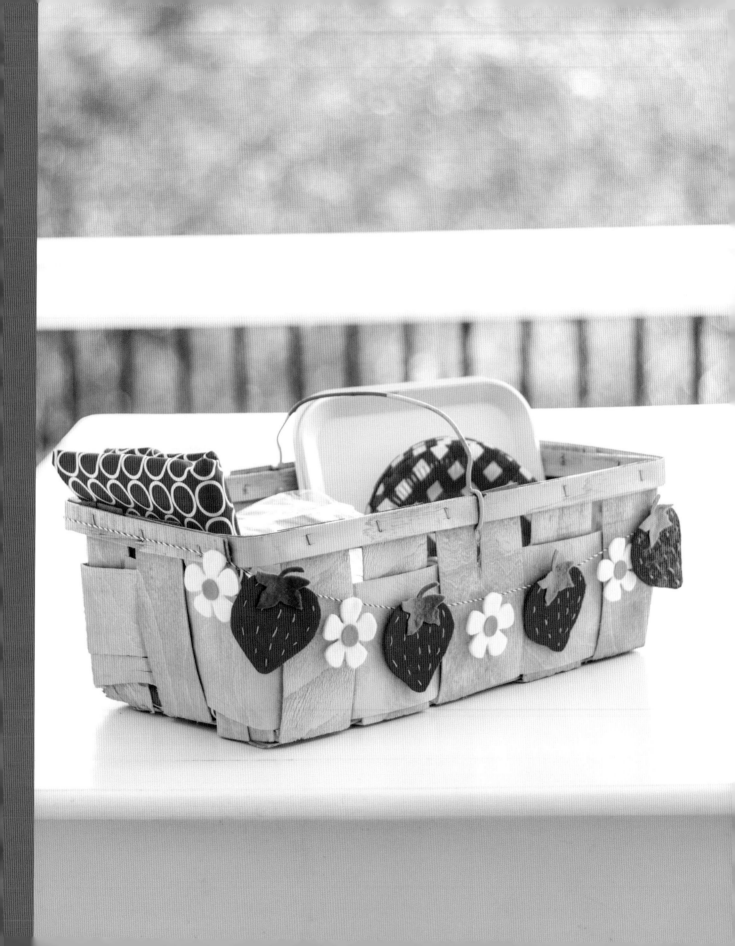

BERRIES & BLOOMS

Nothing signals summer like fresh strawberries! Stitch a sweet row of berries and blooms on baker's twine.

DESIGNER: KATHY SHELDON

WHAT YOU NEED

* Basic Banner-Making Kit (page 2)
* Templates (page 105)
* Felt: red and white, 9- × 12-inch (22.9 × 30.5 cm) sheet for each color
* Felt scraps: green and orange
* *Optional:* freezer paper, pencil, and iron
* Orange embroidery thread
* Fabric glue
* Red-and-white baker's twine
* Needle

WHAT YOU DO

1. Use the templates to cut eight strawberries from the red felt, ten blossoms from the white felt, four leaves and stems from the green felt, and five circles from the orange felt. An easy way to do this is to trace the templates onto freezer paper and iron the paper (waxy side down) onto the felt. Cut through the freezer paper and felt at the same time, then remove the paper.

2. Using the orange embroidery thread, straight stitch the seeds on the front of the strawberry shapes. Place each embroidered strawberry face up on top of a second strawberry and glue them together. Set aside to dry. Once dry, trim around the edges to remove any excess from the back shape if needed.

3. Glue five pairs of the blossom shapes together and set those aside to dry. Again, once the glue has dried, trim around the edges to remove any excess from the back shape if needed.

4. Glue a leaf and stem to the top of each strawberry and set it aside to dry.

5. Glue an orange circle to the center front of each blossom and set it aside to dry.

6. Thread the red-and-white baker's twine through the needle and then take one long stitch through the top back of each piece, starting and ending with a blossom. Hang your garland and think spring!

OILCLOTH CHAIN

Want a garland that can stand up to the outdoors? This so-easy-a-kid-can-make-it oilcloth chain fits the bill.

DESIGNER: DANA WILLARD

WHAT YOU NEED
* Basic Banner-Making Kit (page 2)
* Oilcloth scraps
* Scissors, or rotary cutter and cutting mat
* Stapler or tape

WHAT YOU DO

1. Collect a stack of your favorite oilcloth prints. Cut the oilcloth into strips that measure 1½ × 9 inches (3.8 cm × 23 cm).

2. Fold the first strip into a loop and staple or tape the ends together (use staples if you want to use your chain outdoors).

3. Add the next loop, inserting it through the first loop, and continue until the chain measures your desired size.

MINI GUMDROPS

Nothing is sweeter than a treat-themed garland. You'll love these little gumdrops, right down to their beaded sugar crystals.

DESIGNER: LAURA HOWARD

WHAT YOU NEED

* Basic Banner-Making kit (page 2)
* Template (page 107)
* Felt: red, orange, yellow, green, and purple (or other bright colors)
* Silver seed beads
* Needle
* Thread in matching felt colors
* Pins
* Toy stuffing
* Narrow white ribbon

WHAT YOU DO

1. Use the template to cut out two gumdrop shapes from matching felt, then turn one piece over.

2. Decorate both gumdrop pieces with silver seed beads, sewing the beads on at random using a double thickness of sewing thread to match the felt.

3. Cut a small piece of narrow white ribbon (approx. 2½ inches [6.4 cm] long) and fold it into a loop. Turn over one of the gumdrop pieces and sew the ribbon loop to the top. Use thread to match the felt and whipstitch, sewing into the felt but not through it, so your stitches won't show on the outside of the gumdrop.

4. Place the two gumdrop pieces together and pin in place. Starting from the bottom corner, sew up around the edge of the gumdrop with whipstitch and matching thread until you reach the bottom edge again—leaving the bottom edge open for stuffing.

5. Stuff the gumdrop lightly with toy stuffing then sew up the gap with more whipstitches.

6. Repeat steps 1 to 5 to create lots of gumdrops in assorted colors.

7. Cut a long piece of narrow white ribbon to the desired length of your garland. Thread the gumdrops onto the ribbon one by one.

SIMPLE SCRAPS GARLAND

Put your fabric scraps to good use with this simple, cheerful garland that stitches up quickly.

DESIGNER: KATHY SHELDON

WHAT YOU NEED
* Basic Banner-Making Kit (page 2)
* Scissors or pinking shears
* Fabric scraps in a variety of prints and patterns (see Note)
* Iron
* Sewing machine
* Thread
* Long needle (such as a tapestry needle)
* String, 2 yards for each strand

NOTE: *Size your garland's flags to work with whatever fabric scraps you have on hand, keeping in mind you'll need about ½ inch (1.3 cm) of extra fabric at the top of each piece for folding.*

WHAT YOU DO

1. Cut your fabric pieces into rectangles of roughly the same size, depending on the scraps you have available. The pieces used in the garland shown were about 3 × 6 inches (7.6 cm × 15.2 cm) each. Part of the charm of this garland is its simple, scrappy look, so don't worry if your sizes vary a bit. If you don't want your scraps to fray, use pinking shears to cut.

2. Fold the top of each rectangle ½ inch (1.3 cm) to the back (wrong) side, and iron the fold (see Tip).

TIP: *If you plan to hang the garland where it will be visible from both sides, use longer rectangles and fold each piece in half lengthwise.*

3. Sew across the top front of each rectangle using a ⅜-inch (1 cm) seam allowance to create a channel at the top where the string will go.

4. Using a large needle, thread the flags onto the string, spacing each evenly.

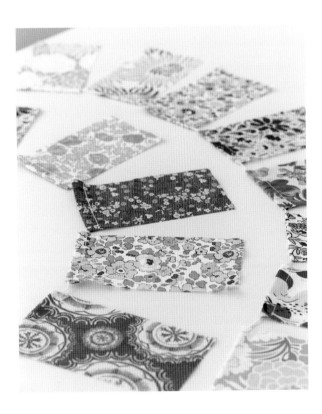

AND MORE

RAINBOW BOBBINS

Cheer up your sewing space with these bright rainbow bobbins.

DESIGNER: LAURA HOWARD

WHAT YOU NEED

* Basic Banner-Making Kit (page 2)
* Template (page 107)
* Pencil
* White card stock
* Eraser
* Glue stick
* Yarn: rainbow colors
* Red and white basker's twine
* Ruler
* Large, sharp sewing needle
* *Optional:* scrap card stock

WHAT YOU DO

1. Use the template and a pencil to draw a bobbin shape on the white card stock. Cut out the bobbin shape, then erase any remaining pencil lines. Use a glue stick to apply glue to one side of the bobbin, covering it completely. Then stick the card bobbin to a second piece of white card, smoothing it flat. When the glue has dried, cut out the bobbin again so you now have a sturdy bobbin shape made from a double thickness of card.

TIP: *Cutting out lots of bobbins? Transfer the template provided onto sturdy scrap card stock to make a template that's easy to trace around and can be reused many times.*

2. Select your yarn color. Tie one end of the yarn around the bobbin, knotting it securely and trimming the loose end. Wrap the yarn around the bobbin, gradually covering the whole central section with yarn "thread." Take care not to wrap the yarn too tightly as it will bend the card. Cut the end of the yarn and knot it in place securely, trimming the loose end.

TIP: *Start and finish your yarn "thread" on one side of the bobbin, so you can hide all the knots at the back of your garland.*

3. Repeat steps 1 and 2 to make lots of bobbins, wrapping each bobbin with a different shade of yarn.

4. Use a pencil and a ruler to mark a small dot at each end of the bobbins, ½ inch (1.3 cm) from the top. Carefully make a hole where you've marked each dot, using a large, sharp sewing needle to poke through the card stock.

5. Arrange the bobbins in rainbow order. Then thread the large needle with a long piece of red and white baker's twine as long as the desired length of your garland and thread the bobbins onto it one by one.

TIP: *Don't have a rainbow of yarn? Use paint or felt-tip pens to color each bobbin, or cut pieces of colored paper or felt to represent the thread.*

POM-POMS IN A ROW

Is there anything more cheerful than a pom-pom? Make a batch in bold colors and string them in a row.

DESIGNER: DANA WILLARD

WHAT YOU NEED
* Basic Banner-Making Kit (page 2)
* Yarn in various colors
* Sewing needle (for stringing pom-poms on to the garland)
* *Optional:* thread or fishing line

WHAT YOU DO

1. Start by making pom-poms (make them all the same size or in various sizes.) Using either two fingers-width (for small pom-poms) or four fingers-width (for larger poms), wrap yarn around your fingers again and again and again, until you've created a large ball around them.

2. When you've wound to your desired "poof," slide the yarn off your fingers and tie a piece of yarn around the center in a knot.

3. Cut through the loops on both sides of the pom-pom. And then give your pom-pom a haircut—trim all the yarn pieces till the pom looks symmetrical and round.

4. Continue steps 1 to 3 to create as many pom-poms as needed.

5. Thread a sewing needle with either yarn, thread, or fishing line. The length of the stringing material should be the desired length of your garland. Push the needle through the center of each pom-pom, stringing them on one at a time, and spacing them as desired.

FLOATING GARDEN GARLAND

String together a collection of small glass bottles with wire and fill your garland and home with fresh blooms.

DESIGNER: KATHY SHELDON

WHAT YOU NEED
* Basic Banner-Making Kit (page 2)
* Wire cutters
* 16-gauge galvanized wire (see step 1 for length)
* Flat-nose pliers
* 9 glass bottles (the ones shown here are 4 inches [10.2 cm] tall)
* 9 flower sprigs

WHAT YOU DO

1. You'll need a large, clear space to work on this garland. Determine the length you want your garland to be and then add an additional 12 inches (30.5 cm) for each bottle you'll be attaching. Use the wire cutters to cut the wire to this length.

2. Starting about 4 inches (10.2 cm) from the left end of the wire, bend the wire to form a small loop for hanging, and then use the flat-nose pliers to wrap the wire tail tightly around the end of the strand. Use the wire cutters to clip the end of the wire if needed.

3. Decide how far apart you want to space your bottles and how much wire you want to leave on each end for hanging. (In the garland shown, the bottles are spaced about 7 inches [17.8 cm] apart with 17 inches [43.2 cm] of wire on each end). Starting at the left end of the wire, place the first bottle in position against the wire. Grab the wire behind the bottle and wrap it around the neck of the bottle twice.

4. Now twist the wire behind the bottle. You can do this by holding the wire tightly with the flat-nose pliers as you bend it, or by holding the main wire in one hand and twisting the bottle upside down and then right side up again to create a twist. If your twist is too loose, use the flat-nose pliers to close up the wire behind the bottle.

5. Continue to work your way down the wire, adding bottles. It will get a bit trickier as you go, but remember that perfection is not what we're after here! The important points are to space the bottles fairly evenly and to make sure the wire wraps and twists are tight enough to hold the bottles securely.

6. Repeat step 2 to form a loop at the right end of the garland. Then carefully hang the garland in place and add water and a flower sprig or two to each bottle.

SEASIDE GARLAND

Display special treasures from your last beach walk with this nautical garland—you'll feel as if you're on vacation every time you look at it.

DESIGNER: KATHY SHELDON

WHAT YOU NEED

* Basic Banner-Making Kit (page 2)
* 2 yards (1.8 m) thick rope
* Pencil or fine-tip marker
* Awl or nail (if using driftwood and starfish)
* Starfish, sand dollars, shells, driftwood, and stones (or other beach finds)
* Hemp twine
* Craft knife with sharp blade or other implement with a narrow-bladed tip
* Vise or clamp
* 2½ yards (2.3 m) thinner rope

WHAT YOU DO

1. Knot each end of the thick rope and then hang it in your workspace with the same amount of bow as you'd like in the finished piece.

2. Use the pencil or fine-tip marker to mark the spot for a hole about ½ inch (1.3 cm) down from the tip of one arm on one starfish. Use the awl or nail to gently poke a hole through the marked spot. Repeat for the remaining starfish. While you have the awl or a nail handy, gently poke a hole through the center of each piece of driftwood. Set the driftwood aside for now.

3. Thread about a foot-long (30.5 cm) strand of hemp twine through the hole in one starfish and secure it with a knot. Loosely secure the other end to the hanging rope (you'll want to be able to adjust how high or low the starfish hang once you've attached all of your objects). Repeat this with the remaining starfish, spread evenly on the hanging rope.

4. Making holes in shells with a drill requires a special drill bit and often results in a lot of breakage. With a bit of patience, you can use a craft knife or other implement with a sharp, bladed tip to make holes with little if any breakage. Use the pencil or fine-tip marker to mark the spot where you want the hole. Mark this on the outside (front) of the shell, so any chips that may occur will be hidden inside (or on the back) of the shell.

5. Secure the shell carefully with the vise or clamp. Place the tip of your craft knife or other implement onto the spot marked, and twist while pushing down gently. Once you've made a bit of a hole to "grab" the knife's tip, blow out any dust and continue twisting the knife while pushing gently until the hole is large enough to thread the hemp twine through it. A bit of pressure and patience are the way to go here.

6. You'll use the hemp twine to string the shells, driftwood, and stones in pleasing groupings. Before adding a piece of driftwood, make a large knot in the twine so the driftwood sits securely. Attach a stone by placing it against the twine and then tightly wrapping another smaller piece of twine around both the stone and the hanging twine and knotting it. Loosely secure each strand of items to the hanging rope. Then adjust all the various strands of the garland so the lengths are pleasing, knot them securely at the top, and clip any excess twine.

7. Wrap the thinner rope loosely around the thicker, main rope and secure it at each end with a knot. Cut any excess.

FLOWER POWER

Hung on a porch or in front of a window, these floating flowers add instant cheer to any space.

DESIGNER: KATHY SHELDON

WHAT YOU NEED

* Basic Banner-Making Kit (page 2)
* Scissors or wire cutters
* Bright yellow and pink silk flowers (9 yellow flowers and 8 pink flowers for each strand)
* Lime green hemp cord
* Large needle

WHAT YOU DO

1. Cut each silk flower from its stem with scissors or wire cutters, making sure you leave enough of the material on the back of the flower so it doesn't fall apart (this may mean you need to leave a bit of the plastic or wire stem).

2. Cut one strand of hemp cord to the length desired plus about a foot (30.5 cm) for excess, then thread the cord onto the needle. You'll need to experiment a bit to find the best way to thread your flowers so they will hang nicely. Generally, a long stitch through the back of the flower to the front (where it should be hidden in the center petals) and then back out through the back will result in the flowers facing straight forward.

TIP: *Try hanging these strands vertically to create a beautiful floral curtain over a window or doorway. Three to four strands of yellow or pink flowers will be enough to grace an average doorframe.*

3. Gently push the flower along the cord until you reach about a foot (30.5 cm) from one end. Keep adding flowers, spacing them evenly until you reach the start of the cord. Hang the strand from a horizontal pole or a nail at the height desired—don't clip any excess cord yet.

4. Continue steps 2 and 3 until you have the number of strands desired. Adjust the flowers as needed by gently sliding them up or down the cords. When you are satisfied with your arrangement, secure the top of each cord to the horizontal pole or nail with a permanent knot, and clip any excess cord at the top and bottom.

COOKIE CUTTER BUNTING

Useful tool or new favorite holiday decoration? Merry up your kitchen with a festive string of cookie cutters in a bold coordinating shade.

DESIGNER: CYNTHIA SHAFFER

WHAT YOU NEED
* Basic Banner-Making Kit (page 2)
* 12 large metal cookie cutters
* 5 small metal cookie cutters
* Apple red glossy spray paint
* 7 yards (6.4 m) gray-and-white baker's twine

WHAT YOU DO

1. Place the cookie cutters on a protected work surface outside. Spray the cookie cutters with quick, even coats. Once the paint has dried, flip the cookie cutters over and spray the other side. Repeat this several times to make sure the cookie cutter is completely covered with the red paint.

2. Cut 5-inch (12.7 cm) lengths of the baker's twine and tie one around the top of each cookie cutter.

3. Cut a 4½-yard (4.1 m) length of the baker's twine.

4. Starting at about 12 inches (30.5 cm) from one end of the baker's twine, tie one of the large cookie cutters to the baker's twine. Tie the next large cookie cutter to the twine, 5½ inches (14 cm) away from the first cookie cutter. Repeat for the next cookie cutter, but this time tie on a small cookie cutter.

5. Repeat step 4 until all the cookie cutters are attached to the baker's twine, ending with two large cookie cutters.

LOS ANGELE

GRANNY'S GARDEN

Sweeten up your space with a simple strand of crocheted granny squares with colorful flower centers framed in white.

DESIGNER: AMANDA CARESTIO

WHAT YOU NEED
* Basic Banner-Making Kit (page 2)
* Scraps of medium yarn, size 4 in color A, and/or scraps in various colors
* Crochet hook: 5.5 mm (size I-9)
* Yarn needle

WHAT YOU DO

1. With scrap yarn, chain (ch) 4; join with slip stitch (slst) in first chain to form a ring.

ROUND 1: Ch 3 (counts as first double crochet [dc]), 2 dc in ring, ch 3, 3 dc in ring, ch 3, 3 dc in ring, ch 3, 3 dc in ring, ch 3, and slst into third ch of beginning chain, pulling through a loop of color A (instead of the scrap yarn).

ROUND 2: With color A, slst to first ch-3 space. Ch 3, 2 dc into ch-3 space, ch 3, 3 dc into ch-3 space. Ch 2, then (3 dc, ch 3, 3 dc) into next ch-3 space. Ch 2 and continue around, until you reach your beginning chain. Slst into the third chain, and fasten off.

2. Repeat step 1 to make more granny squares. Weave in all the ends.

3. With color A, ch 35, leaving about 10 inches (25.4 cm) of unstitched yarn tail. *Ch through the top corner of one granny square, ch 3, ch through the center space, ch 3, ch through the other top corner, ch 7**. Repeat the steps from * to ** to add the other granny squares to the bunting. After you add the last square, ch 35, again leaving about 10 inches (25.4 cm) of unstitched yarn tail.

4. Tie a knotted loop at each end of the bunting for hanging.

IN THE PINES

Celebrate winter with this classic pinecone garland. Simply gather mini pinecones from the yard and paint their edges with a bit of white paint.

DESIGNER: AMANDA CARESTIO

WHAT YOU NEED
* Basic Banner-Making Kit (page 2)
* Small pinecones
* Foam brush
* White acrylic paint
* White yarn
* Tapestry needle

WHAT YOU DO

1. Remove the pinecones from their branches if needed, leaving a little bit of stem at the top.

2. Using a foam brush, paint the edges of each pinecone with white paint. Let dry for one hour.

3. Cut a 10-inch (25.4 cm) piece of white yarn. Wrap the yarn around the stem, knot it twice, and tie a bow with the excess. Repeat for each pinecone.

4. Cut a strand of white yarn to the desired length of your garland. Tie a knotted loop in one end and thread the other end onto the tapestry needle.

5. Pass the tapestry needle through the wrapped yarn (from step 3) and knot the pinecone in place. Attach the other pinecones in the same way, spacing them about 4 inches (10.2 cm) apart.

RAINING ROSE PETALS

Suspended midair with clear monofilament, rose petals make a soft and fluttery descent.

DESIGNER: KATHY SHELDON

WHAT YOU NEED
* Basic Banner-Making Kit (page 2)
* Spool of 8-pound monofilament or fishing line
* Needle
* Silk rose petals (see Note)
* Masking tape
* Curtain rod or horizontal pole
* Hot glue gun and glue

NOTE: *Silk roses are available in the bridal section of craft stores or online.*

WHAT YOU DO

1. Leaving the monofilament on the spool (so it doesn't tangle), thread its end through the needle. Thread 20 to 25 petals onto the line by poking the needle straight up through the back of each petal.

2. Cut the monofilament to the length desired (each strand shown is about 6 feet [1.8 m]) adding about 1 foot (30.5 cm) for excess. Put masking tape on the bottom of the strand to keep the petals from slipping off.

3. Temporarily secure the strand to a horizontal pole, such as a curtain rod. Tape the bottom of the monofilament strand to the floor or weigh it down by tying it to something like the roll of masking tape.

4. Slide all of the petals into the positions desired on the strands—it will look most natural if you vary the distance between groups of petals, clustering some. Don't worry if the petals slip out of position for now.

5. Starting with the top petal, hold the petal in place and carefully add a dab of hot glue to the back of the petal and the monofilament (see Tip). Repeat with the rest of the petals down the length of the strand, remembering to vary the distance between petals for the most natural look.

TIP: *Nothing says crafty like a hot glue gun, but those little threads of glue left behind are so annoying! They are caused by pulling the nozzle away too quickly, so to prevent them, squeeze out your glue, wait a couple of seconds, dip the nozzle back into the glue just a bit, and then pull away. If you still end up with glue threads, pick them off by hand or use a blow dyer on a low setting to carefully melt them away.*

6. Repeat steps 1 to 5 to make as many strands of falling petals as needed. The strands can tangle easily, so to transport them to their final location, carefully wrap each strand around a long cardboard tube, taping each end to the tube as you start and finish and taking care not to crush the petals as you wrap the strands. If you are hanging the petals in an outdoor location, you may need to add small weights to the end of each strand to keep lines from blowing about and tangling.

BUBBLE BUNTING

Let this rainbow-hued bunting add a happy note to any occasion, and then invite your guests to join in and celebrate. Who doesn't love blowing bubbles?

DESIGNER: KATHY SHELDON

WHAT YOU NEED
* Basic Banner-Making Kit (page 2)
* Small paper cups (one for each color)
* Washable liquid watercolor (see Note)
* Toothpicks or coffee stirrers (for mixing)
* Miniature bubble bottles (see Note)
* Dropper or small spoon
* String, twine, ribbon, or cord of your choice
* Butterfly paper punch (make sure butterfly includes a body)
* White vellum
* Hot glue gun and glue

NOTE: *Miniature bubble bottles are sold with wedding supplies or online. Washable liquid watercolor is available at school supply stores, many craft stores, and online. If you use this instead of food coloring (and use only small amounts to make pastel colors), any stains from bubbles popped on clothing will wash out. Make the banner without adding coloring if your celebration involves a precious wedding dress or fabrics such as satin.*

WHAT YOU DO

1. Decide the number of colors (or shades of colors) you'd like your garland to have and set out one paper cup for each color. Add water to fill each cup and a small drop of the liquid watercolor. Play around, mixing colors with toothpicks or stirrers until you have all the shades you want (they will be lighter once you add them to the bubble solution).

2. Uncap the bubble bottles and use the dropper or small spoon to add a drop of the colored water to each bubble bottle (the project shown called for one larger drop for each darker shade and one small drop for each lighter shade). Be sure to wash the dropper or spoon between colors. Recap the bubble bottles and arrange them in the order you want to hang them on the garland.

3. Cut string to your desired garland length, plus excess for hanging. Then cut a 12-inch (30.5 cm) length of string to attach each bottle.

4. Hang your main garland string securely with the desired amount of bow in it. Then attach the 12-inch (30.5 cm) pieces of string evenly down the length of the main string by tying a simple knot in the middle of each short string. Each string will now have two 6-inch (15.3 cm) strands hanging down.

5. Starting at one end of the garland, and with your first bubble bottle in grabbing distance, use the two strands of the first short string to attach the bottle by its neck to the main string with a tight bow. Clip the bow ends to desired length. Repeat with all the bottles.

6. Use the butterfly paper punch to punch butterflies from your vellum. Fold the wings of your butterfly up, leaving the body part flat.

7. Use the hot glue gun to attach the butterflies to the tops or sides of the bubble bottles.

SHRINK PLASTIC BUNTING NECKLACE

It's hard to know which is more fun: watching the shrink plastic shrink down into tiny pennants or wearing a party around your neck when you're done!

SHRINK PLASTIC BUNTING NECKLACE

DESIGNER: KATHY SHELDON

WHAT YOU NEED

* Basic Banner-Making Kit (page 2)
* Templates (page 115)
* Pre-roughened shrink plastic
* Pencil
* Fine-tip black permanent marker
* Colored pencils: red, blue, green, and yellow
* ¼-inch (0.6 cm) hole punch
* Oven or toaster oven
* Parchment paper
* Baking sheet
* Flattener (smooth heavy object, such as a book)
* Sealer (clear nail polish, acrylic sealer, or acrylic varnish)
* Jump rings
* Two 6-inch (15.2 cm) silver chains
* Lobster clasp
* 2 flat-nose pliers

NOTE: *Shrink plastic shrinks to about one-third its original size and becomes nine times as thick when heated. It's safe to bake in your oven. Shrink plastic is magical and easy and a bit unpredictable, so experiment with some simple single-colored pieces before drawing the more elaborate ones. Children will love this project, but high temperatures are involved, so be sure to provide adult supervision.*

WHAT YOU DO

1. Preheat your oven, following the shrink plastic manufacturer's instructions. (The project shown was baked at 325°F [163°C].) Place the shrink plastic, rough side up, over the templates and trace the border of the bunting shapes in pencil. Use the fine-tip black permanent marker to trace the interior designs (or make your own doodles—just remember that you're drawing on the rough back of the shrink plastic, and designs will be reversed when viewed from the front, shiny side).

2. Use the colored pencils to fill in the designs using the photos for reference or using the colors of your choice. Colors darken and deepen when the shrink plastic is heated, so make the colors quite a bit lighter than desired in your finished necklace.

3. Cut out each bunting shape. Then use the hole punch to carefully punch one hole in each top edge of each bunting shape. Don't get too close to the edges or so far in that a jump ring won't fit once the plastic shrinks.

4. Place the decorated pieces, colored side up, between two pieces of parchment paper on the baking sheet, and bake according to instructions. Watch carefully, and don't freak out when the plastic shapes start to wiggle and distort—give them enough time and they should settle back into their original shape, only much smaller and thicker!

TIP: *If you're very sensitive to fumes, use a toaster oven outdoors on a dry day.*

5. When the plastic is shrunk and flat, carefully remove the hot baking sheet from the oven and press down on the parchment-covered pieces with your flattener. Allow the pieces to cool completely.

6. Seal the back (colored) sides of your necklace with the sealer of your choice.

TIP: *Test your sealer first on a scrap piece of plastic that has been decorated with the same colored pencils and baked to make sure the two are compatible—some sealers can cause the colored pencils to run.*

7. Once the sealer has completely dried, attach the buntings with jump rings (see the Tip). Then attach one length of chain to each side of the buntings with jump rings. Use a jump ring to attach the lobster clasp to one end of the chain, and then attach one final jump ring to the other end of the chain.

TIP: *Jump rings are the secret to quick jewelry making. Never pull the ends apart to open one or you'll distort and weaken the ring. Instead, use two pairs of flat-nose pliers to grasp each end of the jump ring and pull one end toward you and the other end away from you, opening just as much as needed. To close the jump ring, reverse the process by twisting the ends back together.*

YARN TASSELS

Make a string of tassels in your favorite shade. Hang these lovelies above your headboard, along a window, or in your favorite reading nook for a pop of saturated color.

DESIGNER: LAURA HOWARD

WHAT YOU NEED

* Basic Banner-Making Kit (page 2)
* Ball of yarn in a color of your choice
* 12- × 6-inch (30.5 cm × 15.2 cm) rectangle sturdy card stock
* Large, sharp needle

WHAT YOU DO

1. Cut two pieces of yarn, each approximately 12 inches (30.5 cm) long, and set aside.

2. Using the rectangle as a template, wrap the ball of yarn around the length of the card template, winding it around the card about 25 times. Wrap the yarn neatly but not so tightly that you bend the card. Then cut the end of the yarn to free it from the ball.

TIP: *Different weights of yarn will result in thinner or fatter tassels (the tassels pictured were made using DK or double-knit yarn). Make a test tassel first, then wind the yarn more or fewer times as needed.*

3. Slide the yarn off the card template, holding the yarn carefully so it keeps its shape. Place the bundle of yarn at a right angle on top of one of the 12-inch (30.5 cm) yarn pieces you cut earlier. Position the piece of yarn so it's in the center of the yarn bundle, then tie it tightly round the center of the bundle and knot it securely.

4. Fold the bundle of yarn in half so the knot is hidden in the center. Then use the other piece of yarn to tie the top of the tassel together. Wrap it around the top of the bundle a couple of times, then knot it securely and trim away the excess yarn.

5. Use scissors to cut the loops of yarn at the bottom of the tassel. Then trim the ends as needed to make the tassel a nice, neat shape.

6. Repeat steps 1 to 5 to make lots of tassels.

7. Cut a long piece of matching yarn in the desired length of your garland and use it to thread a large, sharp needle. Thread each tassel onto the yarn one by one, threading the needle through the small loop at the top of each tassel (created in step 3).

RIBBON MINI BUNTING

Scraps of washi tape or ribbon are all you need to make this mini bunting.

DESIGNER: KATHY SHELDON

WHAT YOU NEED

* Basic Banner-Making Kit (page 2)
* Various washi tape or ribbon scraps (see Tip)
* 24 inches (.6 m) string (per strand)
* Glue
* Clamps
* *Optional:* pinking shears
* 2 chopsticks or wood skewers

WHAT YOU DO

1. Cut short lengths of ribbon, place them right side down under the string, add a coat of glue, and fold each ribbon over the string onto itself. Clamp the fold as the glue is drying so the ribbon is secured to the string.

2. Once the glue has dried, clip the ribbon ends to the length desired, adding a zigzag to some with pinking shears, cutting straight across others, and clipping a V into some with scissors.

TIP: *You can use colorful ribbon scraps in place of the washi tape for an alternate texture.*

3. Tie each end of the string onto the top of a chopstick or wood skewer. Now you are ready to decorate a cake, a pie, or even a potted plant with your cheerful little bunting.

TIP: *Use this mini bunting as a festive touch atop a birthday cake. The possibilities are endless!*

HEART STRINGS

Simple crocheted hearts dance and sway on a single strand of baker's twine. Hang this mini garland anywhere as a sweet sentiment.

DESIGNER: AMANDA CARESTIO

WHAT YOU NEED

* Basic Banner-Making Kit (page 2)
* Medium yarn, size 4 in color A and scraps in color B
* Crochet hook: 5.5 mm (size I-9)
* Baker's twine
* Embroidery needle

WHAT YOU DO

1. Using color A, crochet six hearts. Begin: Chain (ch) 3, join with a slip stich (slst) in first chain to form a ring.

> **ROUND 1:** Ch 3, then 2 double crochet (dc), 3 single crochet (sc) in ring. Ch 1, dc in ring, ch 1, 3 sc, 2 dc in ring. Ch 2, slst in ring, and fasten off.

2. Cut six 5-inch (12.7 cm) strands from color B. Fold the strands in half, and push the loop from front to back through the loops of the bottom dc stitch, at the point of the heart. Pull the ends of the strand through the loop and tighten.

3. Cut a strand from the baker's twine in the desired length of your garland and thread it onto the embroidery needle. Stitch the hearts onto the needle, working through one top edge of the heart, then the center, then the other top edge.

4. Space the hearts evenly along the strand. Tie a knotted loop in each end of the twine for hanging.

BEADS & ORGANZA GARLAND

If you'd like to add a bit of twinkle to your tree or mantel, try this simple beaded project.

DESIGNER: KATHY SHELDON

WHAT YOU NEED

* Basic Banner-Making Kit (page 2)
* ¼-inch-wide (0.6 cm) ivory organza ribbon
* Beading needle (see Note)
* 8 mm × 10 mm green faceted Aurora Borealis (AB) beads (about 7 beads for each foot of garland)
* *Optional:* dental floss (see Tip)

NOTE: *Experiment to see if you have a needle with an eye large enough to accept the ribbon but small enough to go through the beads. If not, see the Tip.*

WHAT YOU DO

1. Cut the ribbon to the length desired for your garland and tie a knot a few inches from the end.

2. Cut the other end of the ribbon at a slant and thread it through the needle. Pass the needle through the hole of one bead. See Tip if you don't have a needle that will accept the ribbon and fit though the hole in the bead.

TIP: *To use dental floss in place of a needle, cut a 3- to 4-inch (7.6 cm to 10.6 cm) length of floss and fold it in half. Thread a few inches (about 7.6 cm) of the ribbon through the bend in the floss and then poke the two ends of the floss through the hole in the bead. Tug on the two ends to pull the floss and the ribbon through the hole and thread the bead onto the ribbon.*

3. Slide the first bead down to about 3 inches (7.6 cm) from the knotted end of the ribbon. Continue threading beads onto, and then sliding them down, the ribbon, spacing them about 1½ inches (3.8 cm) apart.

4. When you've added the last bead, leave about 3 inches (7.6 cm) and knot the end. Cut a notch into both ends of the ribbon.

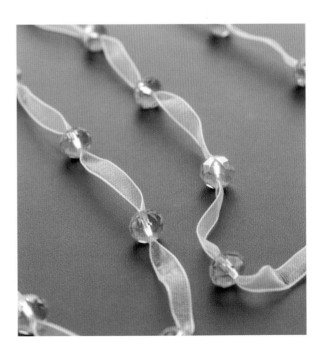

A B C
D E F
G H I

ABC BUNTING
PAGE 19—COPY AT 150%

ABC BUNTING
PAGE 19—COPY AT 150%

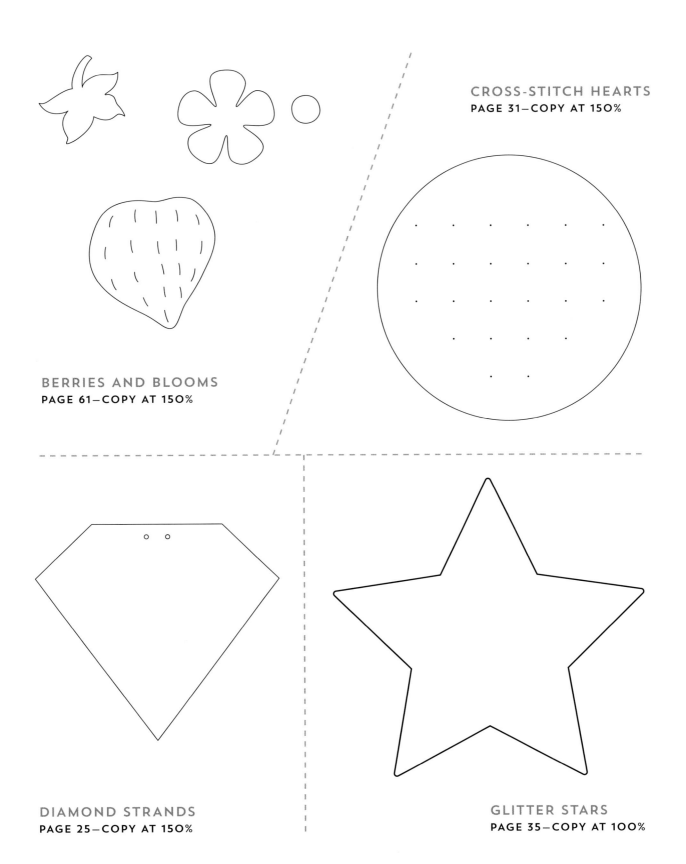

CROSS-STITCH HEARTS
PAGE 31—COPY AT 150%

BERRIES AND BLOOMS
PAGE 61—COPY AT 150%

DIAMOND STRANDS
PAGE 25—COPY AT 150%

GLITTER STARS
PAGE 35—COPY AT 100%

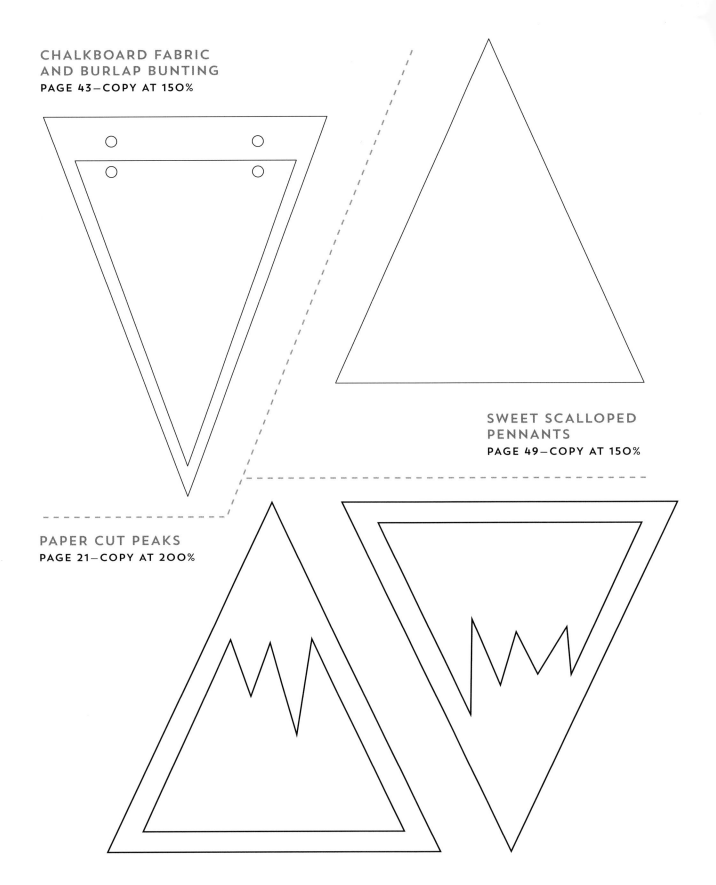

CHALKBOARD FABRIC
AND BURLAP BUNTING
PAGE 43—COPY AT 150%

SWEET SCALLOPED
PENNANTS
PAGE 49—COPY AT 150%

PAPER CUT PEAKS
PAGE 21—COPY AT 200%

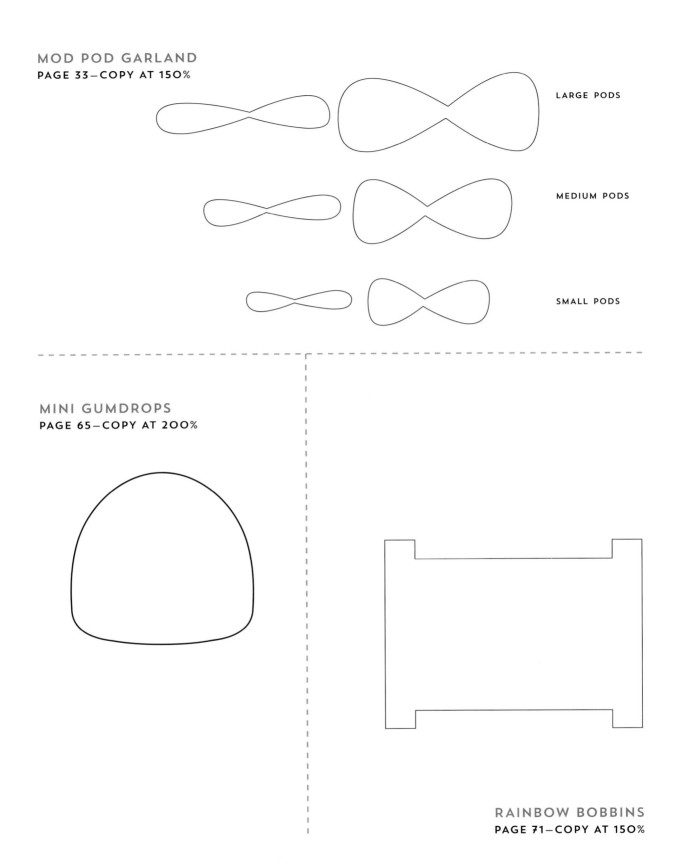

MOD POD GARLAND
PAGE 33—COPY AT 150%

LARGE PODS

MEDIUM PODS

SMALL PODS

MINI GUMDROPS
PAGE 65—COPY AT 200%

RAINBOW BOBBINS
PAGE 71—COPY AT 150%

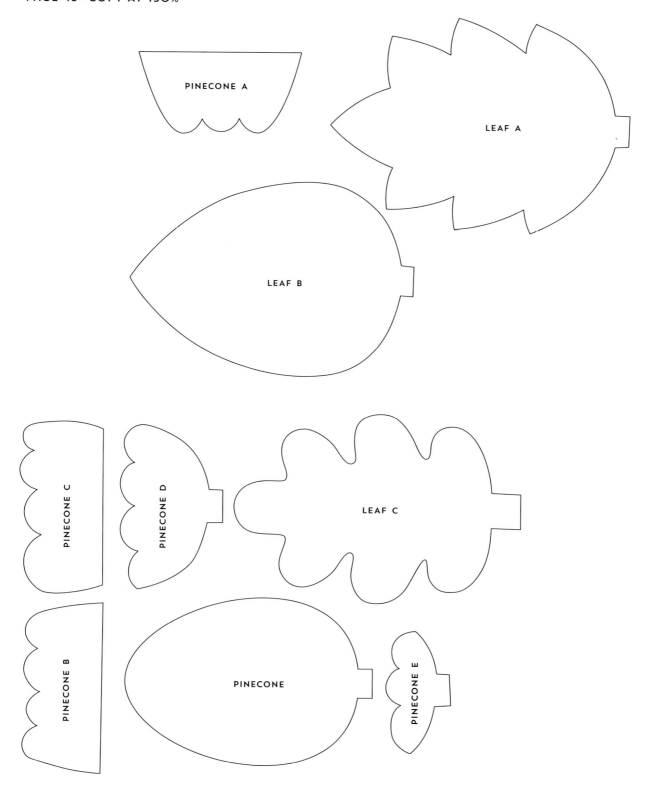

PINECONE A

LEAF A

LEAF B

PINECONE C

PINECONE D

LEAF C

PINECONE B

PINECONE

PINECONE E

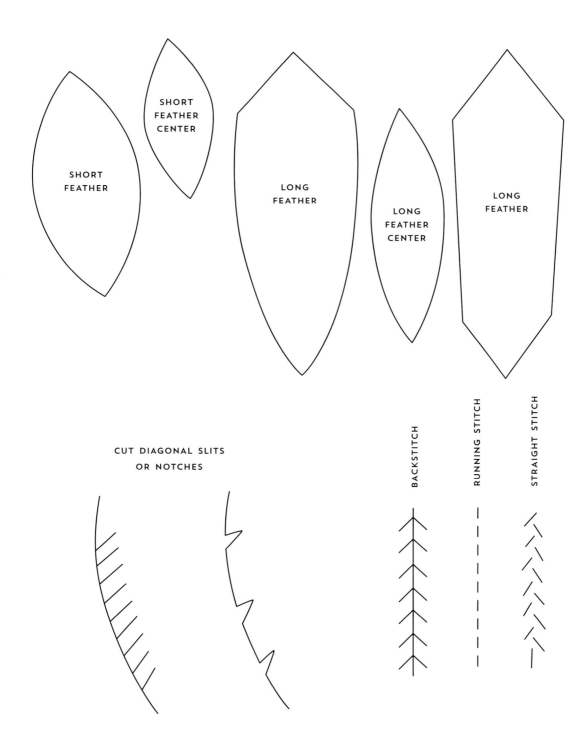

SHORT
FEATHER

SHORT
FEATHER
CENTER

LONG
FEATHER

LONG
FEATHER
CENTER

LONG
FEATHER

CUT DIAGONAL SLITS
OR NOTCHES

BACKSTITCH

RUNNING STITCH

STRAIGHT STITCH

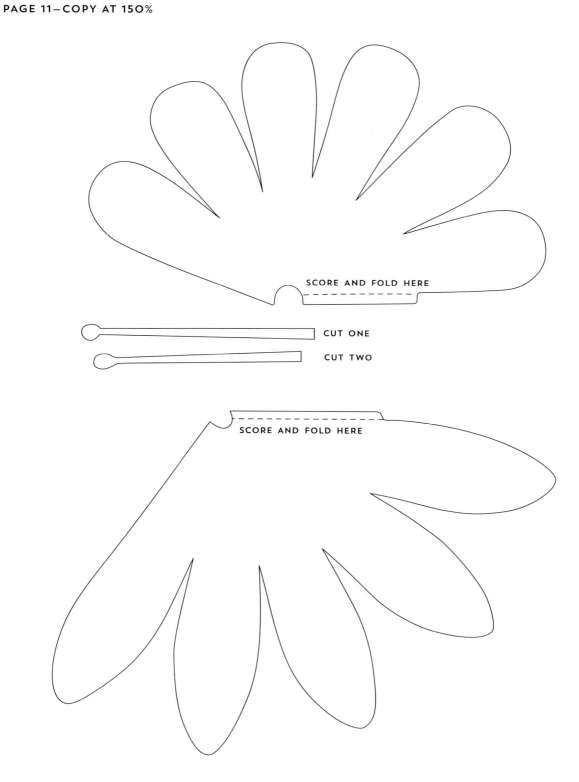

SCORE AND FOLD HERE

CUT ONE

CUT TWO

SCORE AND FOLD HERE

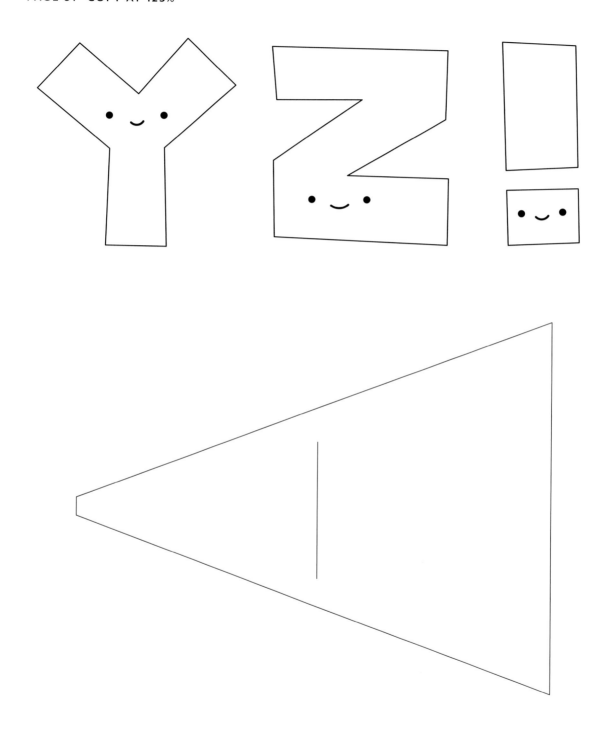

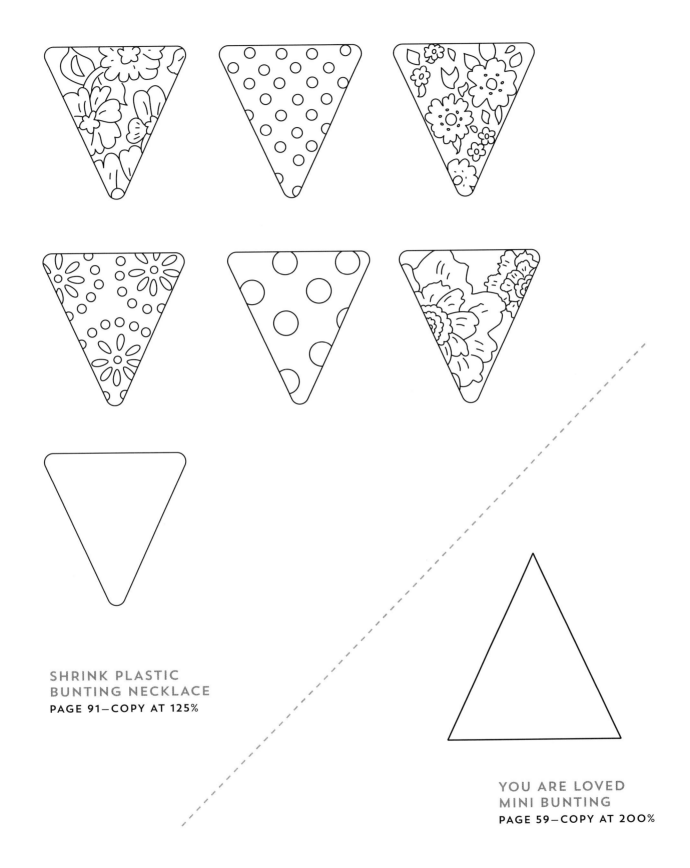

**SHRINK PLASTIC
BUNTING NECKLACE**
PAGE 91—COPY AT 125%

**YOU ARE LOVED
MINI BUNTING**
PAGE 59—COPY AT 200%

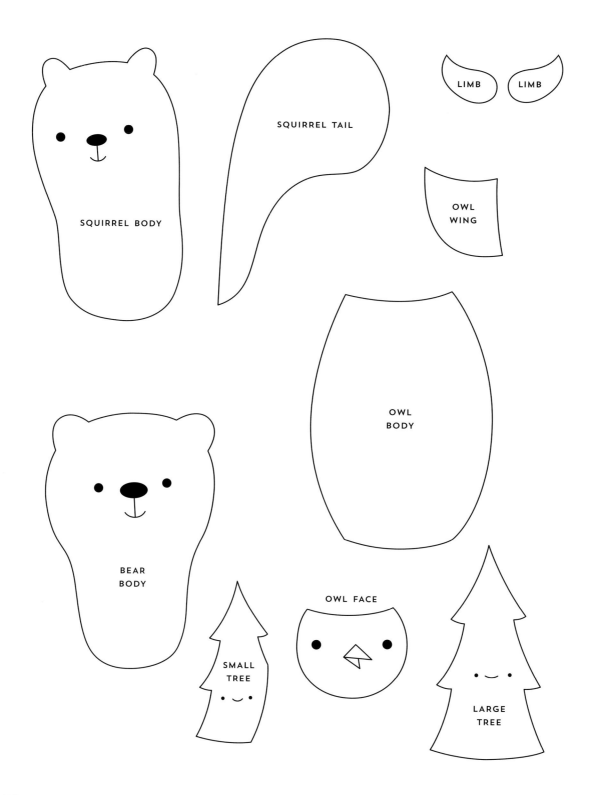

SQUIRREL TAIL

LIMB   LIMB

OWL
WING

SQUIRREL BODY

OWL
BODY

BEAR
BODY

SMALL
TREE

OWL FACE

LARGE
TREE

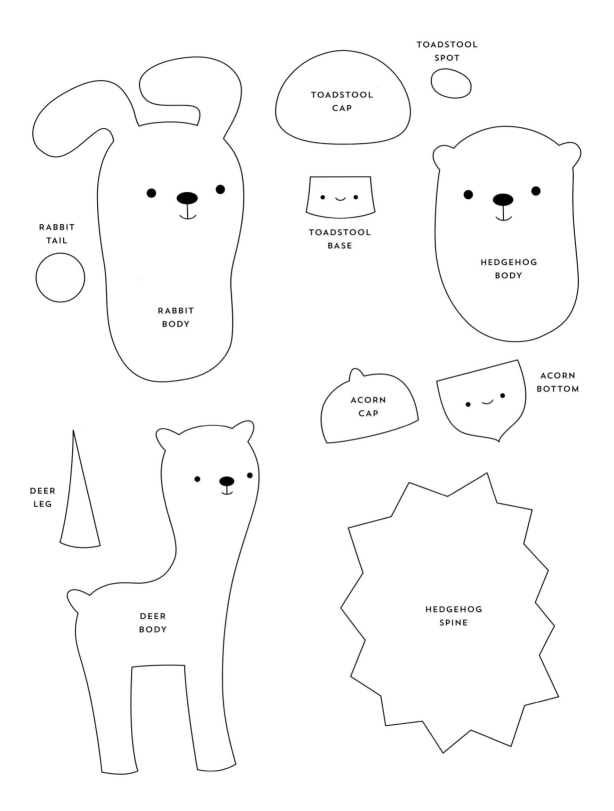

RABBIT TAIL

RABBIT BODY

TOADSTOOL SPOT

TOADSTOOL CAP

TOADSTOOL BASE

HEDGEHOG BODY

DEER LEG

DEER BODY

ACORN CAP

ACORN BOTTOM

HEDGEHOG SPINE

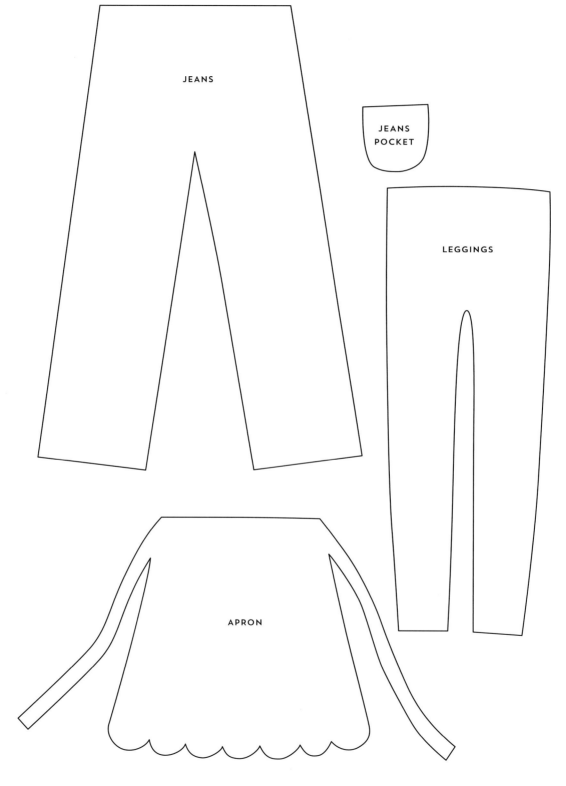

JEANS

JEANS POCKET

LEGGINGS

APRON

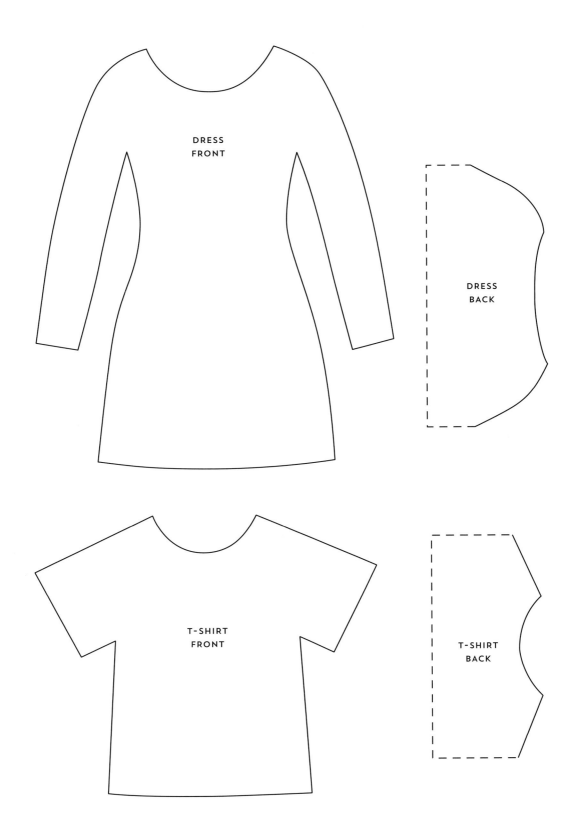

DRESS
FRONT

DRESS
BACK

T-SHIRT
FRONT

T-SHIRT
BACK

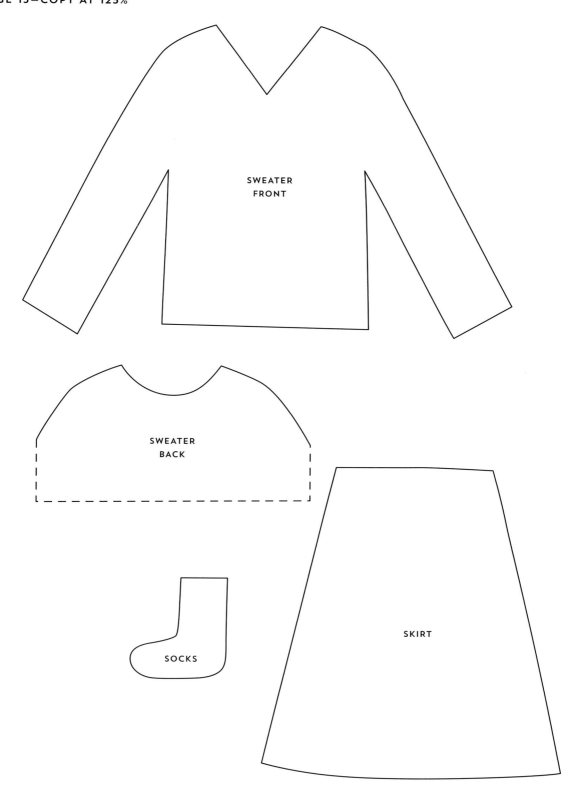

SWEATER
FRONT

SWEATER
BACK

SOCKS

SKIRT

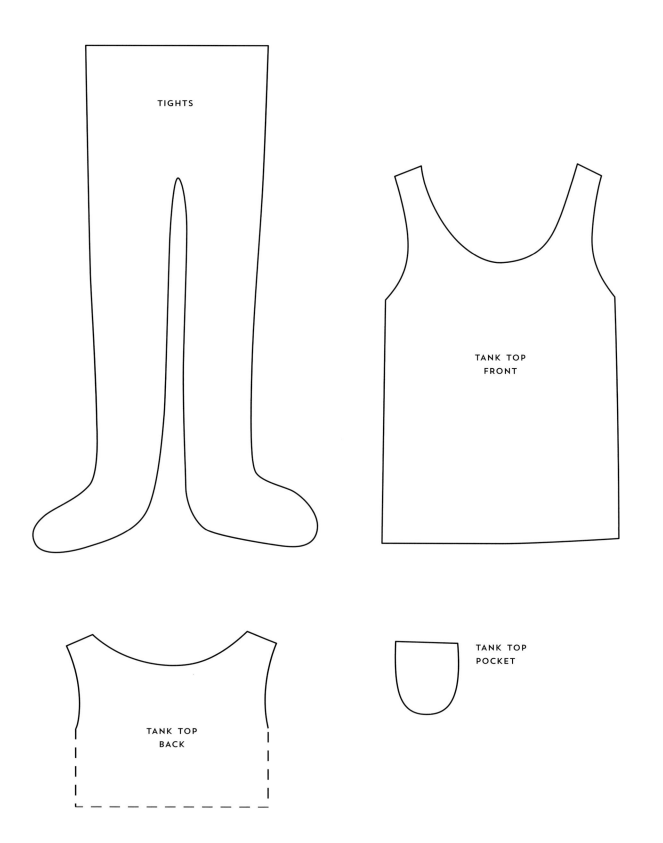

TIGHTS

TANK TOP
FRONT

TANK TOP
BACK

TANK TOP
POCKET

CATHE HOLDEN

Cathe Holden is a craft and design blogger, creator, and instructor who designs, shares, and teaches unique and original projects from her Petaluma, California, studio, Inspired Barn. On her blog, JustSomethingIMade.com, Cathe shares how-to tutorials, free digital designs, and loads of inspiration for do-it-yourself enthusiasts of all skill levels. She is the proud wife of a firefighter and the mother to three wonderful teenagers.

LAURA HOWARD

Laura is a designer/maker and crafts writer who likes to make and do. She designs crafty projects for books and magazines and is the author of two books about felt crafting: *Super-Cute Felt* and *Super-Cute Felt Animals.* Laura shares free tutorials and writes about her crafty adventures on her blog BugsandFishes.blogspot.com.

JENNIFER JESSEE

Inspired by vintage fabrics, magazines, and cookbooks, Jennifer Jessee has been creating fun, stylish retro designs for more than 25 years. Her illustration work can be found in a wide variety of publications in the United States and abroad, including *Wired, Spin, Mademoiselle,* and *Atlantic Monthly.* You can see Jennifer's work at JenniferJessee.com.

MOLLIE JOHANSON

Mollie Johanson has loved creating and crafting cute things for as long as she can remember. She is the author of *Stitch Love: Sweet Creatures Big & Small,* and contributed to *Heart-Felt Holidays* and *Felt-o-ween,* as well as other Lark Crafts titles. Mollie lives near Chicago and is happiest with a cup of coffee, some stitching, and her family close at hand. Visit her at MollieJohanson.com.

AIMEE RAY

Aimee Ray loves all types of arts and crafts and is always trying something new. Besides embroidery, she dabbles in illustration, crochet, needle felting, sewing, and doll customizing. Aimee is the author of *Doodle Stitching, Doodle Stitching: The Motif Collection, Doodle Stitching: Embroidery & Beyond,* and *Doodle Stitching: The Holiday Motif Collection,* and is the co-author with Kathy Sheldon of a book on making jewelry: *Aimee Ray's Sweet & Simple Jewelry.* In addition, she has contributed to many other Lark titles. You can see more of her work at DreamFollow.com and follow her daily crafting endeavors at LittleDearTracks.blogspot.com.

CYNTHIA SHAFFER

Mixed-media artist, creative sewer, and photographer Cynthia Shaffer's love of art can be traced back to childhood. At the age of six, she was designing and sewing clothing for herself and others. After earning a degree in textiles from California State University, Long Beach, Cynthia worked for 10 years as the owner of a company that specialized in the design and manufacture of sportswear. Numerous books and magazines have featured Cynthia's art and photography. She's the author of *Stash Happy Patchwork, Stash Happy Appliqué, Coastal Crafts,* and the co-author of *Serge It!* Cynthia lives with her husband, Scott, sons Corry and Cameron, and beloved dogs Harper and Berklee in Southern California. Visit Cynthia online at CynthiaShaffer.typepad.com or CynthiaShaffer.com.

DANA WILLARD

Dana Willard authors the popular DIY sewing and design blog DanaMadeIt.com and is the host of *MADE Everyday,* a fresh, new sewing show that gives a relatable voice to modern sewing. Her designs and photography have been featured in multiple creative books, magazines, online communities, and in award circles. Her book *Fabrics A to Z* is essential for any sewist new and old. Dana lives in the hot city of Austin, Texas, with her husband and three kids.

ABOUT THE AUTHORS

KATHY SHELDON

Kathy writes, edits, and packages books. She grew up on a farm in New England, so making things by hand comes naturally to her. She's happiest when creating, whether it's a shrink plastic necklace, a poem, a row of sweet peas, or a book about gardening or crafts. She is the author of many books, including *Shrink! Shrank! Shrunk!: Make Shrink Plastic Jewelry,* and the co-author of *Fa la la la Felt, Heart-Felt Holidays, Felt-o-ween, 'Tis the Season to Be Felt-y* and *Aimee Ray's Sweet & Simple Jewelry.* When Kathy is not writing or creating in the mountains of Asheville, North Carolina, you can usually find her at her cottage in Maine, where she's the first to jump in the lake in the spring and the last one to leave the water in the fall.

AMANDA CARESTIO

Amanda's latest crafting obsessions include crocheted hats, half-square triangles, and (still) fusible web. When she's not bent over her sewing machine, at the craft store, or exploring the Blue Ridge Mountains, Amanda enjoys spending quality time with her hubby, two sweet kiddos, and her little brindle shadow, Violet. Amanda is the author of *Wee Felt Worlds* and *Never Been Stitched* (and other titles from Lark Crafts), and co-author of *Fa la la la Felt, Heart-Felt Holidays, Felt-o-ween,* and *'Tis the Season to Be Felt-y.* Her designs appear in many Lark Crafts books.

INDEX